Prisoners Are People

Macklyn W. Hubbell

Dedication

This book is dedicated to the prisoners who have served as research sources and who have written and shared personal and familial information voluntarily and without identification. The cooperation and consent has been for one purpose to help others recognize that prisoners are people.

Acknowledgments

I am deeply indebted to our nephew, writer, artist, and editor, Steven Macklyn Hubbell for his committed editorial work on this manuscript as well as designing the cover of this book. My deep appreciation goes to Margaret Frisbee for typing the "Families of Origin" written by the prisoners themselves. And, of course, my wife, Bet, typed the rest of the manuscript and added helpful editorial comments. For her devotion and professional expertise, I cannot thank her enough.

Table of Contents

Introduction

All people, my faith says, are created in God's image.

Is this image ever erased?

Can people do something or be something which eradicates God's image in us?

What about people in mental institutions, are they less than human?

What about violators of the law who are tried in court and found guilty and incarcerated, does this reduce or eliminate their God-likeness?

Does the degree of their violation nullify their kinship to God?

If the answers to these poignant questions are "yes", who determines this?

If the answers to these questions are "no", why do we treat some people as if the answers are "yes?"

Seeing men wearing circles of black, green, or red on their trouser legs either in a prison setting or outside the "fence" on a work assignment stimulates fear in most or many people. The observers think without documentation that they are all wild killers or child abusers. Some are, of course; but by and large they are like everybody else except they have been apprehended, tried in a court of law, found guilty of a felony, and sentenced to serve in prison—a sentence of time based on the law.

I must admit that I, when I began my research in the Pre-release Center at Parchman in the 1970s, was a bit apprehensive about my being locked up in a hall or classroom with men wearing circles on their pants. However, after working day by day and year after year, I realized that they were and are people like all other people outside the Parchman fence. To be sure, they were caught, tried, and sentenced to serve in the penitentiary for a specified length of time. Notwithstanding, they are people made in God's image.

Decades after my doctrinal program and study in the 1970s, I was invited by the New Orleans Baptist Seminary in 1999 to teach college courses at the Parchman site to qualify the inmates to receive a baccalaureate or associate degree. Since then, I have taught these men courses ranging from Introduction to Counseling to Conflict Management.

In my earlier days of teaching, there were those prisoners who tried to manipulate me: "Call the governor for me" or "Bring me this or that." They learned, however, that I could not be used legally or otherwise.

In the spring semester of 2015, I unfortunately developed a blood clot in my right lung causing me to be hospitalized for three days and to miss my scheduled classes at Unit 30. When the prisoners were told about my brief illness, they, with the encouragement and guidance of the prisoner coordinator, Bruce Silk, signed a card entitled, "A Healing Prayer" and sent it to me.

The card read:

> *I am lifting you up with a prayer that you'll be healed. Hold on to*
> *God's promises no matter how you feel. I pray you receive a touch*
> *From the Lord. You are on my heart daily. Trusting that you will be*
> *Restored.*

The printed verse was impressive; but it was their signatures following messages that they wrote that reinforced my opinion that "prisoners are people."

The following messages, handwritten on the card were:

> *There is healing in the Great Physician's hands. I love you*
> *in Christ. Be healed in Jesus' name.*   *Michael*
>
> *The black guy Ronnie loves you.*
>
> *God bless. Get well.*   *Henry*

Remember, the Lord is your shepherd, and He's watching over you and will restore you soon. Hoping to see you soon.   Barksdale

Get well, Professor, soon. We are expecting you back in class. We have a book to finish out there.   Randy

I recovered. You will, too.   David

May God bless.   Randal

What's up, Doc? You get well. OK? You got that? Stay away from cocoa leaves.   Wesley

Love ya!!   Mack

Hurry up and get well. We miss you.   Donnie

Get well soon.   W.

Our prayers are with you.   ROW

Wishing you a speedy recovery. Your captive audience. Get well soon.   Charles

I hope you get well soon.   Alan

All from the FBI—Faith Based Initiative. We love you, Doc Hubble.

My knowledge of these prisoners and the tone of their messages support my heartfelt premise that prisoners are indeed people.

Chapter 1

Incarcerated People

Incarcerated people at the Mississippi State Penitentiary are given an identifying number, outfitted with trousers with circles of black, green, or red or an orange jump suit and housed behind metal fences. These men have been found guilty of offenses by criminal courts which have specified penalties determined by the court system of Mississippi.

They are confined as punishment for their violations. Underlying punishment by law may be an attempt to rehabilitate or restore—if they are "lifers" or if they complete their sentences and are released. No matter what their offenses, they are still people who have come from families and, in most cases, are connected loosely or tightly with their extended families. A recognition of their personhoods is often denied or ignored by civil society.

These men are not the only persons who are considered less than people by the outside world. Persons in mental institutions with diagnoses like schizophrenia are likewise considered below the line of personhood. And in some cases, persons with handicaps either physical or mental and who are not confined to either an institution or hospital may be considered less than people.

The New Orleans Baptist Theological Seminary has introduced an academic and rehabilitation program consisting of offering college courses allowing inmates to work and receive either a two-year associate degree or a four-year bachelor's degree in Christian ministry.

For more than sixteen years, I have been teaching courses which inmates can apply to their chosen degree program: Introduction to Counseling, Abnormal Psychology, Addiction counseling, Conflict Management, etc.

The program prepares them for release or for leading a Christian life within the penitentiary. When released, they return to their communities. For the "lifers", their lives will consist exclusively of a life behind the fence. They are taught to accept reality and serve as Christians where they live—in prison.

In the process of my professional training, I have had the opportunity of working in mental institutions in both Kentucky and Mississippi. As a graduate student at the Southern Baptist Theological Seminary in Louisville, Kentucky, I worked as "an intern" in a mental institution. Many memories are stored in my cognitive bank. Two, in particular, stand out; one brought "tears" another brought "smiles." In the former category was a patient who lived in a manic state. Because of his elevated state of mind, a sadistic attendant delighted in using him as a punching bag. When the attendant was not involved in routine duties, he sought this patient out to punch him with his fists. This was pathological behavior on the part of the attendant, I felt. I decided to report him to a medical officer in charge of the ward. He agreed and requested that I report my observations to the clinical board, which I consented to do if I could sit across the table from the accused as I gave my report. The result was the attendant was immediately terminated. This experience brought on tears for both the attendant and the patient for both were persons made in God's image.

The other occasion was that of an elderly schizophrenic patient who had an inflated view of his worth. One afternoon he requested private time with me. When we walked over to the corner of the ward, he extended his hand offering me a "play" aluminum coin saying, "This is a million dollars; I want you to have it." This brought on internal smile.

As part of my doctoral internship, I spent a semester living at the mental hospital for veterans in Gulfport, Mississippi. I slept in the professional quarters, but I ate and counseled with the patients. I lined up in the "chow line" and made my way serving my plate. One noonday I was standing between two patients. The one in front of me said he was Billy Graham and the one behind me said that he was General McArthur. No matter what their mental states, they were persons.

Over the years I have continued to relate professionally with marginal persons. As a professor I, along with my colleagues, counseled with inmates at Angola, a Louisiana State Prison. When violators in Cleveland, Mississippi, were either fined or incarcerated for violations, I presented to the municipal judges and aldermen a plan to establish a trash program to keep the city clean and to allow violators to work off their fines. From Monday through Friday, I meet and have met with the offenders to give them credit for hours worked and make street assignments for the next day.

As a part of my Ph.D. studies, I chose to research and write my dissertation on this published title: <u>A Study of the Treatment of Group Counseling and Psycho-drama at the Pre-Release Center for Men, Mississippi State Penitentiary.</u> As the title indicates, I conducted group counseling and psychodrama over a period of twenty-one days. The intent of the study was to prepare these men for life after their release from prison. They were given the Kahn Test of Symbol Arrangement (KTSA) prior to the program (pre-test), at the conclusion of the program (post-test), and post-wait test, a test administered wherever they were after their release—Mississippi, Tennessee, Alabama, etc. To my disappointment, I had to accept my null hypothesis—no change as a result of the pre-release program.

No matter what the offense or state of mind, they are all persons deserving respect as human beings. People are people!

In prisons, in mental institutions, and in the world at large, persons have emotional problems. Many end up incarcerated, hospitalized, or wander unrelated to reality. Less than human? No!! Persons are persons.

Macklyn W. Hubbell

Chapter II

A Walk Through

After I clip on my staff ID badge, I head east on Highway 8 from Cleveland and north on Highway 49W in Ruleville, it is just a matter of 15 minutes before I turn left at the gate which leads to the Parchman Penitentiary. A guard exits the guard house to identify me and all others who approach the gate with its signed overhang. She will visually identify my clipped-on badge and the sticker on the windshield of my automobile. I say "She" because more females than males are guards at this all male prison. When I started my work at Parchman in the 1970s, female guards were few and far between. Not so now. The reason is simple: guards must be 18 or older and must not have had criminal records. Unfortunately, many or most male applicants have prison or jail records which make them ineligible.

Once I have passed inspection, the metal gate is electronically pulled back allowing me to enter the prison grounds. For the first few meters, I am allowed to travel 20 miles per hour; then the speed limit is increased to 30. My destination is Unit 30 located in the interior of the prison along with 5 other units in the second area. Only Unit 29 (maybe minimum security) is located in the first area.

Upon arriving at and entering the designated parking lot for Unit 30, I park and enter another inspection area. In this area are more female guards who require that I put all detachable personal items (shoes, belt, wallet, etc.) in a plastic basket to be x-rayed. As my personal items are examined, I pass through a machine which x-rays my whole body. Then I am examined by another guard who directs me to sit in a chair which x-rays me in a sitting position.

By this time, my personal items in the plastic trays have passed approvingly on a conveyer belt; and I am free to put my personal items on like my shoes and belt and put my wallet, pens, etc. into my pockets. When I pass this inspection and have repossessed my personal items (except automobile keys which are kept until I have completed my teaching), I leave this security area and pass outside through a metal gate into open space. Since there are no guard towers, a double fence surrounds Unit 30 and a patrol car moves slowly around the unit to discourage attempts at escape or to detect any irregularity in the compound.

Next comes another security station. With female guards behind a secured area controlling the metal doors, I step inside one door. The guard closes the door behind me. Now I am between two locked doors, an area about the size of a closet. When the guards are satisfied that I pass muster, I am allowed to exit from this security building to open spaces,

For about 100 yards, I walk to the next building called the holding tank. Entering this building where the prisoners who have been outside Unit 30 are stopped and searched, I exit another metal door and take ten steps before identifying myself to a guard who opens still another metal door—the entrance (finally) to my classroom area.

Fifty or so prisoners are seated at tables prepared to hear my lectures and take notes. With a microphone attached to my lapel, I begin teaching. Often I leave the lectern to move among the prisoners dressed in their black or green ringed trousers. The black ringed prisoners have fewer privileges than those wearing the green.

For three hours, except for lunch break, I teach courses like sociology, psychology, and counseling. These courses and other courses are offered according to the academic cycle. Some of the prisoners are auditing and others are taking my courses and other required courses to fulfill the academic requirements for either the associate or baccalaureate degree.

Like most other academic settings, the eager, receptive students sit at tables in the front of the classroom. This rectangular classroom is approximately 75'X200'. Students who choose not to be called on or identified usually sit from the center to the rear of the classroom. I will walk from front to back and side to side as I teach. In my professional wanderings, I lecture and observe their note-taking. By this way, the female guard will enter the classroom and calmly walk from table to table observing their behavior and attentiveness. Most inattentiveness comes from the rear of the classroom. An example of one who was not paying attention was a young man who was incarcerated because of murder. With crossed arms, he sat at his designated space. He was not taking notes; just staring in my direction. I made it a point to approach his table. Whenever I saw what appeared to be the slightest interest on his part, I would say, "George, do you want to comment on what I have just said?"

Sometime, he responded hesitantly. Over the semester, however, he opened up. At the end of the semester, he presented to me a painting of snow falling on trees and a house. I observed that the painting was bright with sunlight and snow indicating a lifting of what appeared to have been depression.

I am not suggesting that this transition occurs among all of the resisting students. Some maintain their resistance indicated by looking sideways with crossed arms. When tests are given, these resisting students will not answer the question or will make a snide response. My attitude remains positive with those who have closed their minds. "You win some and you lose some."

The only break in my three-hour lecture comes when the guard announces, "Going back," which is a term for "chow time." Often I will follow them to the next building to observe them eating lunch. Even as they pass through the "chow line" and take their assigned seats, I am observing the behavior of all of the prisoners, but especially the "classroom registrants."

When my period has ended, I walk out of the classroom to sign out in the guards' office area. I had signed in and now I am required to sign out. My exit from the classroom back to my parked vehicle does not require scrupulous inspections. As I drive back to the entrance gate, I attempt to obey the speed limits (20 and 30 mph). Leaving the compound does not require any special protocol—only an examining peek in the trunk of my vehicle. Then I turn south on Highway 49W, returning to Cleveland.

Chapter III

Prison Subculture

In time and with experience, people develop a way of living and/or thinking; and then they transmit this from one generation to another. This is referred to as "the culture of a group of people." There are those in a culture who develop a way of living which is distinctive enough to distinguish it from the overreaching culture. This is referred to as a "subculture."

In some cases subcultures develop as a result of "powers that be." For instance, when African Americans before and after the Civil War were not allowed to be integrated into the culture, they were forced to develop their own subculture—dialect, style of life, etc. Another example involves persons who commit felonies, are tried and convicted in a court of law in Mississippi, and are sentenced to serve in the state penitentiary at Parchman. Because of their confinement, prisoners have developed their own prison subculture. (By the way, some statistics report that there are more than two million incarcerated persons in the United States and 25% of all imprisoned in the world.)

Although the personnel responsible for maintaining control and safety within the prison are employees, not incarcerated by court decisions and confined by law, they do constitute and contribute to the structure in which the incarcerated live, contributing to the prison subculture. Removed from daily lives of the prisoners, but influential in the maintenance of the system, is the Department of Corrections with personnel like the commissioner and superintendent. On the premises of Parchman are the captains and lieutenants whose dress identifications are white shirts and blue trousers; and those dressed in blue shirts are those ranked below those in white shirts.

Unofficially there are groups composed of prisoners who "qualify" to be a part of their chosen gang. According to the prisoners themselves, the names of the gangs at Parchman are: Vice Lords, Gangsters, Royals, Arian Brotherhood, and Latin Kings. Gangs have a relationship with themselves and certainly relationships with other prisoners as well as with the prison management. For the gang members themselves there is a protective element. They band together or align with each other to protect themselves from non-gang members as well as other groups. With what they consider to be their strength or power, they will use this unidentifiable source as pressure to gain favor or special positions in places like the yard, dorm room, or dining room. Since gang members have the perception of strength, they will wield this with or against guards, other prisoners, or management in general. Basically the gang members create fear in general and negative consequences in particular among both management and prisoners.

Privacy or lack of privacy is a pervasive concern of prisoners themselves. Their dormitory style quarters consist of row after row of double deck bunks. Even when they retire in bunks, space between does not block out either body odors or noises. Securely located above their sleeping quarters, toilets, and showers are guards in enclosed and secure areas. These security pens allow the guards—male and female—to view prisoner activities at all times. Obviously this means that toilets and shower activities are visible at all times to both fellow prisoners as well as guards. The only private possessions of the prisoners are boxes located at the head of their bunks. Of course, the contents are restricted to personal items and are subject to inspection by security at any time.

This lack of privacy is understandable and necessary for security reasons—safety for the prisoners themselves as well as safety for the institution. This visibility of the prisoners and proximity of fellow prisoners at all times, including lining up person to person for movement to the dining room, classroom, or elsewhere, violates their innate sense of personal space; but this observation of a lack of privacy is in no sense a negative criticism of this prison system or any other; after all, personal freedom is one of the privileges prisoners lose upon conviction and incarceration. Among other losses are voting, carrying arms, certain monetary benefits forfeited during incarceration, being with or seeing family members (except on days of visitation), and the registration of sex offenders—to mention some of the losses of personal privileges. For a period of time, legitimate spouses were allowed conjugal visits; but for reasons known only to management, these were discontinued.

Language in Parchman's subculture has developed over time with prior generations. Upon being asked to write commonly used prison words, the following were some of their responses:

Wham whams and zoo zoos – sweet cakes and candy

Count time – time for head count

Rack down – get on your bunk for head count at bed time

Spice – marijuana type drug

Roll – a self-rolled cigarette

Barn yard pimps – chickens

Wolf booty – baloney

Pumpkin head – been beat up

Snitch – to squeal

Free world – outside

Toothpick – a small joint

Tonk – conjugal visit

Hit man – one to kill or take out

Deuce it up – form columns on the sidewalk

Shake down – search of property

Love truck – canteen

Crack action – get beat.

Newly incarcerated prisoners may have left a subculture in their city or town. The characteristics of a subculture in the "free world" may have similarities to those at Parchman; but the subculture at Parchman has developed over time and is different from outside subcultures. The bottom line is that new prisoners are expected to accept the existing Parchman subculture. The consequences of not accepting the way things are "could have dire consequences" for the prisoners.

As long as prisoners are at Parchman, they must conform to prison expectations. The length of the sentence may be multiple years or multiple lifetimes. However long they remain confined, the subculture is their culture.

Chapter IV

Shared Insights

The teaching program at Parchman has obvious pluses—for the prisoners as well as the teachers. For the prisoners, they have an opportunity to learn intellectually and grow emotionally. Semester by semester, classes which meet academic standards, provide academic satisfaction on the parts of the prisoners. Once they have passed the course and once the academic value of the courses adds up, the sum total is an associate degree or a baccalaureate degree. Of course, there are those persons who take courses without plans to achieve either of these goals. Self- improvement may have been their only goal or they may have viewed classes offered and accepted as an opportunity to alter the routine of prison life. And there are those prisoners who want to achieve academically or be enhanced personally who see learning as an opportunity of growth as well as an opportunity to share what they have received with their fellow prisoners—"an opportunity of service."

As a teacher in the system over the years, I have had the opportunity to develop relationships. This allowed me the privilege of getting to know prisoners as persons. Consequently a level of trust has developed over the years. Because of this trust, I have been able to invite them to share their inner feelings and thoughts.

To gain additional credit for them and to ferret out their inner private thoughts, I invited them to respond to these questions:

1. What brought you here? (meaning, to prison)

2. What have been the most difficult adjustments you have had to make?

3. How can you make the most out of your confinement?

Macklyn W. Hubbell

SURVEY I RESPONSES

1.) <u>What brought you here?</u> Greed/Covetousness : I broke into a man's house with the intentions of stealing his money and ended up killing him in the process.

2.) <u>What has been your most difficult adjustment here?</u>

Trying to be a follower of Christ in this environment. Dealing with the loneliness that accompanies the incarcerated, though surrounded by people, and having to experience more of it as I confess Christ as Lord. (Nobody wants to talk to me — including family — about Jesus.)

3.) <u>How can you make the most positive contribution to prison life?</u>

By helping men who come here cope with their surroundings. See the things in their lives that are destructive habits, and helping them get rid of those habits and replace them with healthy ones (by means of encouragement, an open ear and a lending hand, and a willingness to "stick by their side" all throughout the process — whether it's losing weight, learning to read, quiting smoking, getting out of a Gang and turning to Jesus, learning their Bibles etc. etc.)

I help men who are close to going home (5 years or less) prepare for the challenges they will face upon release by helping them overcome their personal struggles and giving them the hand of fellowship so sought out for in this place.

By showing mercy & kindness toward those everybody else hate.

① What brought you here?

The sales and manufacturing of meth got me in trouble with the Law, but wrong family values, wrong thinking about self and God are the root causes.

② What has been your most difficult adjustments here?

The breaking up of my family (my son and his mother) is the most difficult adjustment, but other adjustments such as tight living space with no privacy, diet and limited control of my own life are difficult to deal with and adjust to.

③ How can I make the most positive contribution to prision life?

I can make the most positive contribution to prision life by fullfilling Gods call on my life to teach and pleach Gods word and to pastor people around me.

① What brought me here to prison:

I was arrested for rape and sentenced to life without parole. I'm guilty and had accepted my situation & stay in this place. I had an unhealthy fixation on white women growing up based on my aunt's rape by two white policemen in 1962. They were found not guilty by a jury (in chicago – not mississippi). The police dept. fired them and the police station's watch commander that was on duty at the jail that night after the trial – but nothing else was ever done to them. My aunt committed (page 2) suicide the day after they were found not guilty.

From the age of ~~16 12~~ 12 until I were arrested in 1980 I was mixed up with racial hate towards white folks — but lusted after white women, because they were attractive & forbidden — and I thought of them as revenge towards white men for my aunt's rape & suicide.

My actions & hate brought me to prison and a wake-up call. I always justified my actions because of my aunt's suicide and the past history of mistreatment of Black women. However, in prison slowly realized that I were just a sick-minded person filled with hate. It wasn't until I got saved March, 2009, that I realized that only Jesus can clean me and forgive me of my past and give me a new life to serve Him & spread the Good news to others.

#2) What has been your most difficult
adjustments here.

Trying to deal with privacy and
adjusting to dealing with 108 individual
in a housing zone.

It can drive you crazy. I still
don't know how I have adjusted to it
after 33 years.

#3) How can I make the most
positive contribution here at Parchman.
After I graduate — I would like
to work with the chapel Dept. and

help other inmates come to Jesus. I would like to hunt some of these youngsters here come to Jesus and serve Him. Get an education & grow spiritually, educationally, and physically — without prison robbing them of their life here.

* <u>What brought you here?</u> Living a life that revolved totally around my wants & desires. I lived free for thirty-three years pursuing every form of adventure, entertainment, & earthly pleasure, never finding true satisfaction. Never knowing that Christ was the one thing I needed. This absence of Christ led to drug addiction, murder, & finally life in prison.

* <u>What has been your most difficult adjustments here?</u>

For me the most difficult thing was confinement. I have always been an avid outdoorsman. Motorcycles, ATV's, snow skiing, mountain climbing, scuba diving, I was always on the go, never in one place for very long. Sort of like a wild animal being caught & caged, it took a long time to learn that Christ was all the adventure I would ever need again. Prayer is my adventure now. I roam the heavens freely with Him now. ☺

* <u>How can you make the most positive contribution to prison life while here?</u>

By submitting my life whole-heartedly to Jesus Christ as a preacher & soul winner.
By learning to live on faith & prayer alone.
By seeking to truly love God with all my heart, soul, mind, & strength, & by learning to truly love people with the love of Christ.
By seeking first God's Kingdom, storing all my treasures in heaven, & learning to let Him have total control over my every thought, word, & deed, & teaching others how to do the same.

1. What brought me here? I was young and on drugs and violated another woman's *personal space*, I actually took something from her, which in the end I was charged with Rape.

2. What has been your most difficult adjustments here?
One of the first difficult adjustments is being away from my family and kids these many years. To see my kids going through emotional and mental pain is difficult, to watch them grow up from prison because of my bad decision making is real difficult. Then, another difficult adjustment is to adjust to my setting and all the different people and personalities. Being around all these guys whose thinking is totally different from what you would call right or moral thinking is challenging. Everybody here is selfish and sees things from only one lense and it is difficult for me because I wasn't raised that way. I haven't got it down yet, after 7½ years I'm still making adjustments.

3. How can you make the most positive contribution to prison life while you're here?
By sharing with the men around me and the ones in passing about the hope of Christ. Share with them the awesome power of God and how He has changed me. I am giving them what their

, , ,

missing and that's hope in Christ Jesus. To help them see the light, as God has brought me to the light.

1. What brought you here? My addiction to sexual sins, lying, stealing. Was convicted on a sex charge. I thank God is a forgiving God. Hopefully I can make it right one day with those I have offended by using what was learned in this class.

2. What has been you most difficult adjustments here? The inmates around me always doing wrong and I'm trying so hard to do right. They are always cursing, smoking and other things. It is hard to maintain living for Jesus sometimes, but he always comes through to help me. Showing me not to be so judgemental, because when I was younger I was the same way.

3. How can make the most positive contribuation to prison life? By showing the love of Christ. Sharing the gospel and using what I learn from the school to others. Hopefully they will accept the help that is given from God's word, and what was learned not only from this class but from all the classes I have attended.

1. What brought you here (Parchman)?

   I was charged, tried, and convicted of capital rape. I was given a life sentence (with parole).

2. What has been your most difficult adjustment here?

   I was aclimated to a military life (active duty USN) when I was arrested. What I found at Parchman is the complete opposite of what I was used to. At Parchman everybody is in charge; but no-one is accountable. The inmate mentality was alien to me in that they seemed to be content with their status.

3. How can I make the most positive contribution to prison life here?

   I try to be a good witness to Christ and to be a model for others to emulate. This must be working because I have close friends in all of the prison organizations who often bring their "problems" to me to help them correct (peacefully) before they have to correct them (forcefully).

   I have counseled with inmates who have lost family members through death. One in particular had a wife with cancer who gave up on treatment — I spent many hours listening to this man in his grief and sorrow, but, when she passed, he was relieved that she was no longer suffering. My military training (Navy chief petty officer) helped me in my counseling endeavors. I can be trusted.

1.) What brought me too Prison?
A problem arising in my life, unlike all the times
before this, I made the wrong decession. I let
anger overtake my mind, and in a fight I
took another person's life. I put myself in Prison.

2.) What has been my most difficult ajustment
in Prison life?
Dealing with the many personality, in Prison I
have too deal with them, and in the free-world
I could leave the presents of them, or not deal with
them. Dealing with lots of people, and many personalitjes.

3.) How can I make a positive impact too
Prison Life?
I can live as best I know how based on
the Bible. In living this way people can see
Jesus in me, and I help fellow inmates and
officers in any way. I do what is right to
God and from my heart.

1. What brought me here? My Pride. I allowed my pride to cause me to not forgive my wife when she left me, and I took her life. Now, I thank God for giving me a heart to forgive and forget, no matter how much it hurt me.

2. What been your most difficult adjustment here? Knowing that I might not never see or be with family, especially during the holidays. I also find it hard to adjust to the privacy I do not have when in the shower or using the toilet. However, pulling my pants down to let another man see my nakiness is worst off all. God's word say that a man shouldn't look upon another man nakiness.

3. How can you make the most possible contribution in parchman? By becoming a license I RA to help spread God's word throughout this falicity by preaching the gospel of Jesus Christ to Christians and lost souls that does not know that Jesus Christ died so that they do not have to continue living in sin hurting themselves, love ones, and others around them

1. What brought you here? I raped a girl because I allowed my urges to get out of control. These desires came as a result of indulging in pornography, which created a lack of feeling for others. I victimized my victim because I had no empathy and did not view here as a person, mearly an object of sex. It was all my fault. I am to blame.

2. What has been your most difficult abjustment here?

Being away from my family is my most difficult adjustment. I have lost many people to death since I have been here, and who knows who else will pass until I am released. It is hard because I was not there for those people when they needed me most. Feeling helpless is my most difficult adjustment

3. How can you make the most positive contribution to prision life?

I can make the greatest contribution by being the man Christ has called me to be. By living my life as an example of the life changing power of God, I can leed others to Jesus who is my Master Healer. Jesus is the greatest thing I have, so my greatest contribution is giving Him away to those who need Him most.

1) *What brought you here?* At a very early age, my parents taught my syblings and I to treat others the way we wanted to be treated. This lesson has been a blessing most of my life up unto year 2004. I found out that trying to be the good neighbour to the wrong kind of people turned this good lesson into a curse. Trying to be a mentor to the antics of a 15 year old Juvenile Deliguent, backfired in the fact I was a victim of lies that was ment towards the teenager basically getting his way. This cost me my freedom because of something I did not do.

2) *What has been your most difficult adjustment here?* Knowing I was put here baised on lies and not being able to see my family. Being a very un-trusting person in the first place, I have hod problems adjusting with prison life in general. With all the corruption that is like a cancer not only here, but throughout MDOC as a whole makes things so difficult. I see things going on knowing they are either forbidden or illegal and those of us who are trying to do what is right, with those violating getting all of the breaks and privaliges. Not only with the penal system but how the Legislature either makes new laws or changes existing laws making it easier for those offenders to be set free from prison.

3) *How can you make the most positive contribution to prison life?* With the personal problems I have had to face my entire life, Polio, sexual abuse, not trusting anyone — including <u>God</u> — I feel the most positive contribution is rising above all of this and be a weapon for God as I slowly learn to put my trust in Him. Also, the most positive influence in my life thus far is the fellowship of F.B.I. any Dr. Hubbell's influence. I'm not there yet - I know I have a very long way to go and I am trying!!! ☺

1. What brought you into conflict with the law?
2. What has been the most difficult adjustments here?
3. How can you make the most positive contribution to prison life?

1. What brought me into conflict with the law? I committed murder and armed robbery. I guess I believe that rebellion in my early formative years from early childhood to my incarceration. I could not deal with failure and rejection in a positive manner. So I dealt with failure and rejection by peers or family in anger or withdrawal. I eventually developed the attitude of I don't care and sought hard to portray this lifestyle even though inwardly I did care. However, I portrayed this as a way to shelter myself from pain of failure and rejection. The person I killed I did not know and he did nothing to provoke me. The anger, pain, frustration it was already within my heart. I guess you can say it was in my anger bag pushed down. Once it's pushed down so far eventually it comes to the surface. I was angry at life because it did not turn out like I expected it. Angry at humanity because I sensed like humanity always kicked me down no matter how hard I tried to achieve what the peer group says was success. I was angry at God because I came to him and was rejected I believed

by him. I believed what a minister said when he stated alledgedly to my parents I did not know what it took to be a minister. So I lashed out at all three through this one man. Crimes against people in my opinion are actions taken against humanity as a whole even though it is directed at one person. We are a family unit regardless of ethnicity, social status, education, etc. and as a child rebels against ones parents the child rebels against the community to express hurt and disapproval of the way they are treated because they can not verbalize how they feel and don't believe anyone's listening anyway.

2. What has been the most difficult adjustments here? I have had to learn to function as a responsible human being without blaming society that I live in for my plight. Dealing with the sense of no worth because of my own actions that brought about my incarceration. How society did not want to deal with the problems I had that brought about my behavior but just cut me out of society like a cancerous tumor and discarded me into an institution. To deal positively with all my past regrets of an unfulfilled life due to my incarceration. Not knowing the appreciation of family until I was severed from them and having the possibility of not being reunited with them before their death. The idea of dying alone in prison without anyone who cares or love me.

3. How can I make a positive contribution to prison life? Maybe there will be one person I encounter that may have similar problems like me. That God can use me as a vessel to reach out to that person and help them in a constructive way that not only brings them into a relationship with God but will also help equip them to live a life to the fullest advantage possible because they learn how to live. Life is precious a gift to be cherished and the saddest part is to see people who have potential to be something great for the Creator and giver of life waste away in prisons and drug abusers destroying themselves and people that love and care about them. I hope and pray with the instruction of scripture the Holy Spirit and some dedication I can reach one person.

1. What brought you to Parchman.
2. What has been the most difficult adjustment here.

3. How can you make the most positive contribution to Prison Life.

(1) A simple Guilty Plea from Pearl River County. My case is complex. I Had No drug problem or any Criminal intent only a dead boy with a gun shot wound to Head. I Had No prior Felonies of any kind at 44 years of Age. I Have an Illegal Sentence and 20 years of Reading the LAW.

2. I have never been subjected to the authoritarian concept of a total slave environment. The idea of No rights for American Citizens is an old idea that has been resurrected by a fictitious that ignores History and the Constitutional Mandates. The idea that one can Not oppress issues in a court of LAW is the Hardest.

3. No the best you can. I was already a Christian and it's Hard Not to Judge the ignorant for what they truly are. I am Now 64 years old and Falling down Fat.

1. WHAT BROUGHT ME HERE?
LOST of Self-Control, I FELT like I HAD been betrayed, USED, AS in TAKING ADVANTAGE of ME by THE PERSON I THOUGHT loved ME THE MOST, WHEN AT THE TIME I WAS being USE AND WHEN I CONFRONTING THE PERSON SHE lAUGH IN MY FACE AND I LOST IT, I COMMITTED AGGRAVATED ASSAULT ON HER AND MURDER ON ANOTHER.

2. WHAT HAVE been MY MOST DIFFICULT ADJUSTMENT HERE?
MOSTLY MISSING MY fAMILY, ESPECIALLY MY KIDS & MOM. ITs HARD ON ME FOR NOT TO BE THERE FOR MY KIDS TO BE TEACHING AND RAISED THEM AS A FATHER SHOULD, BUT I ALSO KNOW THAT IT HURTS THEM, SO I DO MY BEST TO ADJUST WITH THEM THROUGH LETTERS, VISITATIONS, AND PHONE CALLS. NOW THE FOOD, NO PRIVACY IN REST ROOMS OR SHOWER AND EVEN THE HARD BED I HAVE TO SLEEP IN, I'VE lEARNED TO BE CONTENT, AND I THANK THE LORD FOR WHAT I DO HAVE.

3. HOW CAN I MAKE THE MOST POSSIBLE CONTRIBUTION TO PRISON life? MY CONTRIBUTION WOULD HAVE TO BE MINISTRY IN All AREAS of PRISON, AND TO SHARE MY TESTIMONY of WHAT CAUSE ME TO BE WHERE I AM NOW IN life, BECAUSE THE CHOICES WE MAKE IN life CAN EFFECT OUR fAMILIES AND love ONES, AlSO THAT CHOICE MIGHT TAKE A FEW SECONDS TO MAKE BUT A life TIME TO PAY FOR IT, I WOULD like TO HELP PEOPLE MAKE THE RIGHT CHOICE IN life.

1) What have I saved?

2) What has been your most difficult adjustment here?

3) How can you make the most positive contribution to prison life while you are here?

1) My lack of self-control brought me here. The absence of the _____ over my lifestyle. I abused alcohol and prescription medication to help cope and escape events in my life which, actually, led to further self-destruction. The impairment of my judgment contributed to putting myself in compromising situations that were against the law. So I suppose the real issue would be my inability to cope and adjust to problems in life along with the lack of God to keep guide, direct and _____ me.

2) There have been many difficult adjustments. The most difficult would have to be the loss of friends and family. While there are many lifestyle adjustments, such as loss of choice, privacy, comforts, etc., survival so-to-speak is not the most difficult. In a sense I go through periods of mourning over loss of friends, family and freedom. Sometimes something as simple as realization of the last time I petted a dog or had a certain favorite food triggers a depressed state. Being alone here is also difficult, most of the time there is little common ground with _____

39

those around me and I feel isolated in a sense. The adjustments are really too numerous to name or discuss here. The realization of loss is probably the most difficult.

3) I hope to continue to follow the leadership and guidance in the Lord. Hopefully, through preaching, teaching, hebrew and example I am point or lead someone to Christ. Lord willing, I will graduate the course and be able to improve my services provide here for inmates through the Chaplains department and volunteer services. I plan to continue my education and contribute as He shall see fit. I may not know what it is, but I must believe that God has a purpose for me and I am here "for such a time as this."

① WHAT BROUGHT YOU HERE?

② WHAT HAVE BEEN YOUR MOST DIFFICULT ADJUST-
MENTS TO BEING HERE?

③ HOW CAN YOU MAKE YOUR MOST POSITIVE CONTRI-
BUTION TO PRISON LIFE WHILE HERE?

① HAVING LIVED WHAT MOST PEOPLE WOULD HAVE
THOUGHT TO BE AN EXEMPLARY, GODLY LIFE MOST OF MY
ADULT YEARS, I BEGAN, IN 2007, TO MOLEST AND
VIOLATE MY ADOPTED TEENAGE DAUGHTER. IN NOVEMBER
2011, SHE COURAGEOUSLY CONFRONTED ME ABOUT IT.
I HAD, AS IT WERE, MY EYES OPENED TO THE ENORMI-
TY AND WICKEDNESS OF MY SIN. I CONFESSED TO MY
WIFE OF 30 YEARS, TO MY DAUGHTER, AND TO GOD.
I DROVE RIGHTAWAY TO THE SHERIFF'S OFFICE,
ENTERED A FULL CONFESSION, AND TURNED MYSELF
IN, BEGINNING THE LONG JOURNEY OF REPENTANCE
FROM SIN AND PURSUIT OF GOD.

② MY MOST DIFFICULT ADJUSTMENT STILL IS THE
RECOGNITION OF MY DEPRAVITY AND SINFULNESS, THE
ACCEPTANCE OF GODS FORGIVENESS, AND THE
CONVICTION THAT HE STILL HAS MUCH WORK FOR
ME TO DO IN HIS KINGDOM. EQUAL IN DIFFICULTY
IS THE INABILITY TO PROVIDE FOR MY FAMILY, HAVING
BEEN A PROFESSIONAL OF ABOVE AVERAGE INCOME

WITH A WIFE WHO LOVINGLY HOME EDUCATED AND WAS A FULL TIME MOM AND SPOUSE. SHE HAS NOW BEEN FORCED TO ENTER THE WORK FORCE TO PROVIDE WHAT IS PROBABLY A VERY SMALL INCOME TO MAKE ENDS MEET. FURTHER, SINCE I AM NOT RECEIVING ANY COMMUNICATION FROM MY WIFE AND FIVE CHILDREN (27, 21, 18, 17, 14 YRS OLD), I DO NOT MENTALLY KNOW HOW THEY ARE DOING DIRECTLY, THOUGH MY PASTOR SAYS THEY ARE COPING WELL AND SEEKING CHRIST.

③ BY SEEKING HARD AFTER GOD, RESPONDING TO HIS GRACE FULLY, AND BY STRIVING, IN HIM, TO FULFILL THE MINISTRY HE HAS CALLED ME TO LIVE! TO HELP OTHERS WHO HAVE NO HOPE, ESPECIALLY THOSE OUTSIDE OF CHRIST' COVENANT OF GRACE. BY HIS AMAZING GRACE, IN THE TWO YEARS I'VE BEEN IN PRISON, HE HAS SOVEREIGNLY USED ME TO ADVANCE THE KINGDOM, IN SPITE OF MYSELF. THE PRIVILEDGE OF BEING A SEMINARY STUDENT AND LEARNING HOW TO BE A MINISTER IS A HUGE BLESSING TO MY SOUL. I SEEM TO BE CALLED UPON DAILY TO USE WHAT GOD HAS TAUGHT ME IN THIS CLASSROOM, AS I LIVE AND MOVE ABOUT IN THE CONFINEMENT OF MY DORMITORY. I HOPE TO SEE MANY MEN BE TRANSFORMED BY GOD AS I SHARE THE GOOD NEWS OF JESUS CHRIST.

Chapter V

More Insights

As set forth briefly in the preceding chapter, the following set of questions were presented to the prisoners for their voluntary response. As in the first set of questions (Chapter IV), the prisoners were fully aware that I would incorporate their responses in <u>Prisoners Are People</u> without any personal identification.

The responses to these fifteen questions will provide the reader with additional insights into the thoughts and feelings of the prisoners. Together with the shared insights of Chapter IV, their answers (in their own handwriting in Chapter V) will offer more insights to their inner thoughts.

Macklyn W. Hubbell

SURVEY II RESPONSES

!. Describe your growing up family. (functional/ dysfunctional)
Christian Family

2. Did you feel wanted by your parents as a child? *Yes*

3. When did you first become a violator of the law? What was the violation?
Homicide / Robbery - age 18

4. Who influenced you the most to become a violator?
Peers

5. Do you consider yourself to be an inferior person because of your imprisonment?
No

6. What are the greatest stressors in prison? *No continuity in rules / No privacy*

7. What do you miss the most being confined? *Personal choices*

8. Do you see a mission purpose while you are in prison? *Yes*

9. If so, what is your mission purpose? *Same Jesus gave to the Apostles*

10. What contacts do you have with your family now? How often do you hear from them or see them?
All are deceased - been incarcerated almost 40 years.

11. Has your family rejected you because of your imprisonment? *Immediate Family - No; Extended Family - yes.*

12. Does your family encourage you now? *No*

13. What part does your religious faith play in your life now? When did it begin? *Controls my life, began in 1986*

14. What was your dominate emotion

In childhood *Happiness*

In adolescence *Happiness*

In adulthood *Anger*

Fear anger hurt happiness hope disappointment

15. What is the most personally disturbing factor in prison? *Corruption amongst staff and prisoners, especially introduction of contraband*

46

Prisoners Are People

!. Describe your growing up family. (functional/ dysfunctional) *functional about 90% of the time. Occasional dysfunction, in the form of domestic violence.*

2. Did you feel wanted by your parents as a child? *yes*

3. When did you first become a violator of the law? What was the violation? *at age 20, Drug distribution*

4. Who influenced you the most to become a violator? *peers in society*

5. Do you consider yourself to be an inferior person because of your imprisonment? *No*

6. What are the greatest stressors in prison? *having to deal with other people*

7. What do you miss the most being confined? *freedom and family*

8. Do you see a mission purpose while you are in prison? *yes.*

9. If so, what is your mission purpose? *education*

10. What contacts do you have with your family now? How often do you hear from them or see them? *I phone them weekly and visit monthly*

11. Has your family rejected you because of your imprisonment? *No.*

12. Does your family encourage you now? *yes.*

13. What part does your religious faith play in your life now? When did it begin? *a vital Part. A few years ago.*

14. What was your dominate emotion

    In childhood *disappointment + fear*

    In adolescence *hope, happiness*

    In adulthood *happiness*

Fear anger hurt   happiness hope   disappointment

15. What is the most personally disturbing factor in prison? *lack of privacy; unsanitary living conditions.*

1. Describe your growing up family. (functional/ dysfunctional)

Said to be Dysfunctional

2. Did you feel wanted by your parents as a child?

Yes, mom died when I was 15.

3. When did you first become a violator of the law? What was the violation?

2010, Domestic dispute

4. Who influenced you the most to become a violator?

No one

5. Do you consider yourself to be an inferior person because of your imprisonment?

Yes, because we are Constantly demeaned by guards of less Social status.

6. What are the greatest stressors in prison?

No privacy, No Freedom, dealing with my child while being locked up.

7. What do you miss the most being confined?

my Daughter, my wife, my dad, Driving my truck, Running my Company.

8. Do you see a mission purpose while you are in prison?

Sometimes I think I may be able to share my experiences and help someone.

9. If so, what is your mission purpose?

To Help people less fortunate than I.

10. What contacts do you have with your family now? How often do you hear from them or see them?

my dad, Sister, daughter, wife and inlaws. my dad weekly, others monthly.

11. Has your family rejected you because of your imprisonment?

my in-laws do somewhat, but my wife has been the one rejecting me most

12. Does your family encourage you now?

my dad encourages me because of his coaching background and my new Court date Coming up.

13. What part does your religious faith play in your life now? When did it begin?

Praying helps to get me thru the day best I can. It begin in 2009.

14. What was your dominate emotion

In childhood — happyness, felt loved.

In adolescence — upset that my mom died, angry, hurt, insecurity

In adulthood — insecure, Co-dependent, depressed, sometimes manic

Fear anger hurt happiness hope disappointment

15. What is the most personally disturbing factor in prison? I owned a big company in the free world and I am Constantly talked down to by staff and treated like Garbage, I am told when to shower, when to eat, and basically treated like a Child. It has put a real dent in my Ego.

Prisoners Are People

1. Describe your growing up family. (functional/ dysfunctional) DYSFUNCTIONAL

2. Did you feel wanted by your parents as a child? SOMETIMES I DID, SOMETIMES I DIDN'T

3. When did you first become a violator of the law? What was the violation? AGE 11 /STEALING

4. Who influenced you the most to become a violator? CHILDHOOD FRIENDS

5. Do you consider yourself to be an inferior person because of your imprisonment? SOMETIMES

6. What are the greatest stressors in prison? NEGATIVE MEN

7. What do you miss the most being confined? FREEDOM TO FUNCTION AS A MAN

8. Do you see a mission purpose while you are in prison? YES

9. If so, what is your mission purpose? TO BE AN EXAMPLE OF CHANGE TO MEN

10. What contacts do you have with your family now? How often do you hear from them or see them? SOME, BUT NOT MUCH. DON'T SEE THEM THAT MUCH

11. Has your family rejected you because of your imprisonment? NO

12. Does your family encourage you now? YES

13. What part does your religious faith play in your life now? When did it begin?
IT GOVERNS MY WAY OF LIVING. WHEN I WAS 29.

14. What was your dominate emotion

    In childhood – ANGER /(FEAR) HURT

    In adolescence – (ANGER)/ FOAR/ HURT

    In adulthood – ANGER / FEAR/ HURT /(DISAPPOINTMENT)

Fear (anger) hurt   happiness hope   disappointment

15. What is the most personally disturbing factor in prison?
THE LACK OF RESPECT MEN SHOW TO EACH OTHER IN PRISON

!. Describe your growing up family. (functional/ dysfunctional) Best of Both world

2. Did you feel wanted by your parents as a child? yes mother did father acted like He did.

3. When did you first become a violator of the law? What was the violation?
A year of ages Burgulary.

4. Who influenced you the most to become a violator?
Cousin

5. Do you consider yourself to be an inferior person because of your imprisonment?
No

6. What are the greatest stressors in prison?
Being away from my love

7. What do you miss the most being confined?
Children + family

8. Do you see a mission purpose while you are in prison?
yes

9. If so, what is your mission purpose?
To tell young people to do the right things in Life stor them away from this place

10. What contacts do you have with your family now? How often do you hear from them or see them?
Good relationship with family see them often / beside Dad.

11. Has your family rejected you because of your imprisonment?
no

12. Does your family encourage you now?
yes my mom, my girl

13. What part does your religious faith play in your life now? When did it begin?
Very important, different between life or death / at the age of 12.

14. What was your dominate emotion

In childhood ~~happiness~~ disappointment

In adolescence Anger, ~~~~~~ Fear

In adulthood ~~~~~~, disappointment, hurt

Fear anger hurt happiness hope disappointment

15. What is the most personally disturbing factor in prison? possibly living the rest
of my life in HERE.

Prisoners Are People

I. Describe your growing up family. (functional/ dysfunctional) functional

2. Did you feel wanted by your parents as a child? Yes

3. When did you first become a violator of the law? What was the violation?
In 2000, Sexual battery, touching of a minor.

4. Who influenced you the most to become a violator? I allowed lust to enter
my life. I am responsible but I was also once a victim too.

5. Do you consider yourself to be an inferior person because of your imprisonment?
Not any more.

6. What are the greatest stressors in prison? noise, smokers, around me.

7. What do you miss the most being confined? Not being able to reside in the mountains
and breathe freedom.

8. Do you see a mission purpose while you are in prison? Yes

9. If so, what is your mission purpose? To become a man of God. To be a useful Instrument
for his use.

10. What contacts do you have with your family now? How often do you hear from them or see them?
With my Daughter, and Aunt every couple of weeks

11. Has your family rejected you because of your imprisonment? Yes my brothers and son have
turned their backs on me.

12. Does your family encourage you now? Yes.

13. What part does your religious faith play in your life now? When did it begin? but more dedicated than I
Being raised in church as a young man I have now returned, have ever been.

14. What was your dominate emotion - Hope

    In childhood - happiness

    In adolescence - courage, fear at times, anger.

    In adulthood - disappointment in myself.

Fear anger hurt   happiness hope   disappointment

15. What is the most personally disturbing factor in prison?
The noise and annoying habits of others around me.

1. Describe your growing up family. (functional) / dysfunctional)

2. Did you feel wanted by your parents as a child?
   Yes

3. When did you first become a violator of the law? What was the violation?
   About 35 Years of Age

4. Who influenced you the most to become a violator?
   streets

5. Do you consider yourself to be an inferior person because of your imprisonment?
   No

6. What are the greatest stressors in prison?
   Being away from family

7. What do you miss the most being confined?
   My daughter and my freedom

8. Do you see a mission purpose while you are in prison?
   Yes, Start A Youth ministry back home

9. If so, what is your mission purpose?

10. What contacts do you have with your family now? How often do you hear from them or see them?
    Every week

11. Has your family rejected you because of your imprisonment?
    No

12. Does your family encourage you now?
    Yes

13. What part does your religious faith play in your life now? When did it begin?
    Big factor • when I first got Saved

14. What was your dominate emotion

    In childhood   — *happiness*

    In adolescence   *happiness*

    In adulthood   — *disappointment but since has changed because of God in my life*

    Fear anger hurt   happiness hope   disappointment

15. What is the most personally disturbing factor in prison?
    Privacy

Prisoners Are People

1. Describe your growing up family. (functional/~~dysfunctional~~)

2. Did you feel wanted by your parents as a child? *No*

3. When did you first become a violator of the law? What was the violation?
Very young   *destruction of property*

4. Who influenced you the most to become a violator? *Family*

5. Do you consider yourself to be an inferior person because of your imprisonment? *No*

6. What are the greatest stressors in prison? *Meaningless rules*

7. What do you miss the most being confined? *Freedom to go and do*

8. Do you see a mission purpose while you are in prison? ~~────────────~~ *yes*

9. If so, what is your mission purpose? *To lead a congregation*

10. What contacts do you have with your family now? How often do you hear from them or see them? *Once a monthly visit*   *month*

11. Has your family rejected you because of your imprisonment? *No*

12. Does your family encourage you now? *Some*

13. What part does your religious faith play in your life now? When did it begin? *almost 5 yrs.*
It is not part but whole

14. What was your dominate emotion

    In childhood *disappointment/hurt*

    In adolescence *uncertanty*

    In adulthood *disappointment*

Fear anger hurt   happiness hope   disappointment

15. What is the most personally disturbing factor in prison?
Separation from my son

Macklyn W. Hubbell

1. Describe your growing up family. (functional/ dysfunctional)

2. Did you feel wanted by your parents as a child? YES

3. When did you first become a violator of the law? What was the violation?
IN TIME OF INCARCERATION/ MURDER

4. Who influenced you the most to become a violator? My Self

5. Do you consider yourself to be an inferior person because of your imprisonment? NO

6. What are the greatest stressors in prison? LACK OF PRIVACY

7. What do you miss the most being confined? Family: CHILDREN, MOTHER, Siblings

8. Do you see a mission purpose while you are in prison? YES

9. If so, what is your mission purpose? To COMMUNICATE WITH people SPIRITUAL
bECAUSE I AM ANTI-SOCIAl AT TIME.

10. What contacts do you have with your family now? How often do you hear from them or see them?
OFTEN ONCE OR TWICE MONTHLY/

11. Has your family rejected you because of your imprisonment? NO

12. Does your family encourage you now? YES

13. What part does your religious faith play in your life now? When did it begin?
STAYING POSITIVE IN MY FAITH WITH GOD/AT YOUNGER AGE but more POSITIVE NOW.

14. What was your dominate emotion

    In childhood – HAPPINESS

    In adolescence – HAPPINESS

    In adulthood – HURT, diSAPPOINTMENT

Fear anger hurt   happiness hope   disappointment

15. What is the most personally disturbing factor in prison?
LACK OF PRIVACY, AROUND peOPLE WITH bAD HygiENE, UNCLEAN living AREA
& bAD food.

Prisoners Are People

!. Describe your growing up family. (functional/~~dysfunctional~~)

2. Did you feel wanted by your parents as a child? *No*

3. When did you first become a violator of the law? What was the violation?
At the age of seventeen. Robbery

4. Who influenced you the most to become a violator? *A friend*

5. Do you consider yourself to be an inferior person because of your imprisonment? *No* • *Sexual immorality Rape charge.*

6. What are the greatest stressors in prison? *Freedom*

7. What do you miss the most being confined? *Family, a comfortable bed, good food, proper toothbrush and ~~toothpaste~~, quietness, privacy.*

8. Do you see a mission purpose while you are in prison? *Yes*

9. If so, what is your mission purpose? *Sharing the Gospel and my talent playing guitar and teaching others to play.*

10. What contacts do you have with your family now? How often do you hear from them or see them? *Sister, my son were writing but stopped. They haven't came to see me because they live in Philly, Pa.*

11. Has your family rejected you because of your imprisonment? *Some have, others have rejected me because of writing or saying thing in the wrong way.*

12. Does your family encourage you now? *No*

13. What part does your religious faith play in your life now? When did it begin? *Continually relying on Christ to see me through all circumstances. This began the day of incarceration.*

14. What was your dominate emotion

In childhood *Not being wanted*

In adolescence *Loss of a father figure*

In adulthood *Being the person the Lord Jesus Christ would have me to be.*

Fear anger hurt happiness hope disappointment

15. What is the most personally disturbing factor in prison? *Not being able to walk some where without being confined.*

Macklyn W. Hubbell

1. Describe your growing up family. (functional/ dysfunctional) A stable family environment with 2 parents

2. Did you feel wanted by your parents as a child? yes

3. When did you first become a violator of the law? What was the violation?
10-11 Shoplifting from wal-mart. Violation in prison for Murder I, Armed Robbery.

4. Who influenced you the most to become a violator?
Peer-pressure, environment such as culture, violent culture. Bullied when I was younger.

5. Do you consider yourself to be an inferior person because of your imprisonment? yes

6. What are the greatest stressors in prison? Knowing that my family needs me and I can not help them. Knowing that the parole board or society will not consider what I've done since my crime and who I am now they will continue to judge me based on my one past deed. Overcrowded prison environment, criminal staff bringing in contraband.

7. What do you miss the most being confined?
My family being able to be with them seeing my child grow up solitude being able to get away from people at times.

8. Do you see a mission purpose while you are in prison? yes

9. If so, what is your mission purpose? To demonstrate to the parole board and society that I want to re-enter society. I demonstrate this through my behavior and classes I've taken. To encourage others to turn from a life of crime and quit wasting their lives in prison.

10. What contacts do you have with your family now? How often do you hear from them or see them?
I do seldom I have had great family support for the last 20 years. At least 4 Times a year, phone calls 2 times or more a month.

11. Has your family rejected you because of your imprisonment?
No.

12. Does your family encourage you now? yes

13. What part does your religious faith play in your life now? When did it begin? My faith has taught me to live above criminal statute tendancies and has helped me turn from crime and realize the insanity of repeated criminal behavior. It has taught me the value of a human being and the value and blessing of life.

14. What was your dominate emotion

In childhood fear, sense of rejection, anger due to being bullied.

In adolescence same sense of inadequacy along with fear and anger

In adulthood regret over past failures depression

Fear anger hurt happiness hope disappointment

15. What is the most personally disturbing factor in prison? That I may never walk out of prison alive. That my family may die before I can be paroled and I will be left alone.

!. Describe your growing up family. (functional (dysfunctional)) *My parents were divorced when I was 1 or 2. They both loved me. I think my mom felt like she missed out on us.*

2. Did you feel wanted by your parents as a child?
Yes and No. My parents both drank a lot. So I spent most of my time with my grandmother

3. When did you first become a violator of the law? What was the violation?
At the age of 32. 1993. Murder

4. Who influenced you the most to become a violator? *Dope dealers.*

5. Do you consider yourself to be an inferior person because of your imprisonment? *No.*

6. What are the greatest stressors in prison? *Morons. Noise.*

7. What do you miss the most being confined? *Freedom. Family. Women*

8. Do you see a mission purpose while you are in prison? *YES*

9. If so, what is your mission purpose? *To help others cope if I can. I find it harder to cope each day.*

10. What contacts do you have with your family now? How often do you hear from them or see them? *letters and phone calls. Visits every now and then.*

11. Has your family rejected you because of your imprisonment? *Never!*

12. Does your family encourage you now? *YES*

13. What part does your religious faith play in your life now? When did it begin? *It keeps me from killing myself and or others.*

14. What was your dominate emotion

    In childhood *lonliness*

    In adolescence *loss*

    In adulthood *loss*

Fear anger hurt happiness hope disappointment

15. What is the most personally disturbing factor in prison? *that humanity has no hope other than Jesus.*

!. Describe your growing up family. (functional/ dysfunctional)

2. Did you feel wanted by your parents as a child? yes

3. When did you first become a violator of the law? What was the violation?
I was accused and convicted March 3, 2009
The crime was sex
4. Who influenced you the most to become a violator? no one just got caught
up in a bad situation

5. Do you consider yourself to be an inferior person because of your imprisonment?
No I don't feel inferior or less than anyone else because I'm in prison.

6. What are the greatest stressors in prison?
Having to put up with so many people in such small space daily

7. What do you miss the most being confined?
I miss my family wife and kids etc. making my own money standing on my own 2
feet.
8. Do you see a mission purpose while you are in prison?
Yes I do because God took what the devil meant for harm and made it good.

9. If so, what is your mission purpose?
To be able to witness to other people and try to lead lost souls to christ

10. What contacts do you have with your family now? How often do you hear from them or see them?
I have a good relationship with my family

11. Has your family rejected you because of your imprisonment?
My wife has but not our kids we are still married and I'm still depending
12. Does your family encourage you now? on God to fix even that
Yes, very supportive

13. What part does your religious faith play in your life now? When did it begin?
My faith is #1, it started when I was young but I back slid

14. What was your dominate emotion

In childhood

In adolescence

In adulthood

Fear anger hurt   happiness hope   disappointment

15. What is the most personally disturbing factor in prison?

Having to accept the fact I had to spend most of my life here

1. Describe your growing up family. (functional/ dysfunctional) I HAD A VERY functional family. VERY STRUCTURED AND REGIMENTED.

2. Did you feel wanted by your parents as a child?
   I FELT LOVED AND WANTED.

3. When did you first become a violator of the law? What was the violation?
   I FIRST BECAME A VIOLATOR IN '85, ARMED ROBBERY

4. Who influenced you the most to become a violator?
   My DRUGGY FRIENDS

5. Do you consider yourself to be an inferior person because of your imprisonment?
   NO

6. What are the greatest stressors in prison? HAVING MYSELF AND PRIVACY DISREGARDED

7. What do you miss the most being confined?
   WIFE, CHILDREN, LIBERTIES.

8. Do you see a mission purpose while you are in prison?
   YES I DO.

9. If so, what is your mission purpose?
   TO BECOME MORE AWARE SPIRITUALLY, AND MORE MATURE

10. What contacts do you have with your family now? How often do you hear from them or see them?
    I AM IN TOUCH CONSTANTLY AND VISIT ONCE A MONTH.

11. Has your family rejected you because of your imprisonment?
    NOT AT ALL

12. Does your family encourage you now?
    YES

13. What part does your religious faith play in your life now? When did it begin?
    I HAS KEPT ME ANCHORED. IT BEGAN AFTER ORIENTATION

14. What was your dominate emotion

    In childhood — UNCERTAINTY

    In adolescence — CONSTANT HOPE

    In adulthood — DISAPPOINTMENT WITH SELF

Fear   anger   hurt   happiness   hope   disappointment

15. What is the most personally disturbing factor in prison?

DEALING WITH HIDDEN AND DISTURBED
PERSONALITIES IN OTHERS, THAT SOMETIMES
COME OUT IN UNEXPECTED AND CONTENTIOUS
WAYS

Macklyn W. Hubbell

!. Describe your growing up family. ((functional) dysfunctional)

2. Did you feel wanted by your parents as a child? *yes*

3. When did you first become a violator of the law? What was the violation?
In 1991 → a traffic ticket

4. Who influenced you the most to become a violator? *drinking alcohol*

5. Do you consider yourself to be an inferior person because of your imprisonment? *NO*

6. What are the greatest stressors in prison? *Being strip search by a male officer*

7. What do you miss the most being confined? *my Family*

8. Do you see a mission purpose while you are in prison? *Yes, the need For people to really know God in their Life.*

9. If so, what is your mission purpose? *To become an Chaplain's IRA to spread the Gospel*

10. What contacts do you have with your family now? How often do you hear from them or see them?
very little, maybe every 2 months

11. Has your family rejected you because of your imprisonment? *NO*

12. Does your family encourage you now? *yes*

13. What part does your religious faith play in your life now? When did it begin? *It has helped me to better understand God and trust Him. In July of 2012 at Delta Correction Facility in Greenwood*

14. What was your dominate emotion

   In childhood → *happiness*

   In adolescence → *a life of unsureness*

   In adulthood → *disappointment with decision i made that cause pain and suffering to family and others I meet*

Fear   anger   hurt   happiness   hope   disappointment

15. What is the most personally disturbing factor in prison? *Having No privacy when taking a shower and eating food that not properly clean or cooked*

Prisoners Are People

1. Describe your growing up family. (functional/ dysfunctional) *Dysfunctional*

2. Did you feel wanted by your parents as a child? *No*

3. When did you first become a violator of the law? *4/7/95* What was the violation? *Accident; court found murder*

4. Who influenced you the most to become a violator? *Ex-wives taking children*

5. Do you consider yourself to be an inferior person because of your imprisonment? *Of course*

6. What are the greatest stressors in prison? *Cramped in with criminals — prisoners & prison staff*

7. What do you miss the most being confined? *Being alone*

8. Do you see a mission purpose while you are in prison? *Yes*

9. If so, what is your mission purpose? *Showing that the highest station for a human to achieve is slave of God.*

10. What contacts do you have with your family now? How often do you hear from them or see them? *Next to none. / Very rare. None but my sister. Except like twice this year from aunt*

11. Has your family rejected you because of your imprisonment? *Of course*

12. Does your family encourage you now? *No*

13. What part does your religious faith play in your life now? When did it begin? *I don't really have anyone but God. When I was seven — 1970-1971*

14. What was your dominate emotion

   In childhood : *Safety - secure : Fear. Hopelessness*

   In adolescence *Safety - security: Fear. Anger.*

   In adulthood : *Fatherhood : Hurt. Anger. Being emotionally torn-apart.*

Fear anger hurt   happiness hope   disappointment

15. What is the most personally disturbing factor in prison? *Everyone in my business. I don't have any alone time; I.e. — Tomato garden after work. I like to be away from people, and I'm packed in with dregs of society.*

1. Describe your growing up family. (functional/ dysfunctional) *My family was functional.*

2. Did you feel wanted by your parents as a child? *My Mother was both father and Mother.*

3. When did you first become a violator of the law? What was the violation?
I was 23 Murder.

4. Who influenced you the most to become a violator?
Actually I had the wrong friends after my mother died.

5. Do you consider yourself to be an inferior person because of your imprisonment?
No, I had once been a gang member and I led hundreds of mins, now I live for christ.

6. What are the greatest stressors in prison?
My greatest stressors is thinking about my family.

7. What do you miss the most being confined?
I miss living with my family. and seeing my children grow up without a father.

8. Do you see a mission purpose while you are in prison?
Many times I see the mistakes that I have made, and would like to give back to the world.

9. If so, what is your mission purpose?
My mission is to give people a chance to know Christ as I have come to know him.

10. What contacts do you have with your family now? How often do you hear from them or see them?
My family stays in touch with me, and prays for my release, and they still love me very much.

11. Has your family rejected you because of your imprisonment?
No, I felt they should have but they didnt, but they held me accountable for what I did.

12. Does your family encourage you now? *My family does encourage me they give me the respect of a family member.*

13. What part does your religious faith play in your life now? When did it begin?
My faith in God is the reason for my hope. without christ I would be lost.

14. What was your dominate emotion

In childhood

In adolescence

In adulthood

I was very disappointed in myself. I had no right to act outside of myself. I wish I had a do over but that is impossible. therefore, I try hard not to disappoint God any more.

Fear anger hurt happiness hope <u>disappointment</u>

15. What is the most personally disturbing factor in prison?
That I cant return home. and show the world my change everyone should know that God can change even me.

*Thank you for asking.
that was a huge help.
that somebody wanted to
know what I feel.*

Prisoners Are People

1. Describe your growing up family. (functional/ dysfunctional) *functional   good family*

2. Did you feel wanted by your parents as a child? *yes   Grandparents raised me*

3. When did you first become a violator of the law? What was the violation? *Auto burgulary*

4. Who influenced you the most to become a violator? *My cousin*

5. Do you consider yourself to be an inferior person because of your imprisonment? *no*

6. What are the greatest stressors in prison? *no privacy*

7. What do you miss the most being confined? *family*

8. Do you see a mission purpose while you are in prison? *yes*

9. If so, what is your mission purpose? *spread Gods word and learn Trades*

10. What contacts do you have with your family now? How often do you hear from them or see them? *some call them one time a month*

11. Has your family rejected you because of your imprisonment? *I think so*

12. Does your family encourage you now? *some what*

13. What part does your religious faith play in your life now? When did it begin? *alot   started in 2006*

14. What was your dominate emotion

    In childhood   *hurt*

    In adolescence   *anger*

    In adulthood   *love*

Fear   anger   hurt   happiness   hope   disappointment

15. What is the most personally disturbing factor in prison? *no privacy*

!. Describe your growing up family (functional/ dysfunctional)

2. Did you feel wanted by your parents as a child? *Yes*

1960 stolen Candy.

3. When did you first become a violator of the law? What was the violation?

4. Who influenced you the most to become a violator? *Peers*

5. Do you consider yourself to be an inferior person because of your imprisonment? *No*

6. What are the greatest stressors in prison? *The Administration Neglect to Evaluate*

7. What do you miss the most being confined? *family*

8. Do you see a mission purpose while you are in prison? *Yes*

9. If so, what is your mission purpose? *To education myself and learn more of my Strength ; Weakness.*

10. What contacts do you have with your family now? How often do you hear from them or see them? *Often*

11. Has your family rejected you because of your imprisonment?

12. Does your family encourage you now? *Yes*

13. What part does your religious faith play in your life now? When did it begin? *first priority, In 1989*

14. What was your dominate emotion,

    In childhood

    In adolescence

    In adulthood

Fear   anger   hurt   happiness   hope   disappointment

15. What is the most personally disturbing factor in prison?

The filthiness

1. Describe your growing up family. (functional/ dysfunctional) *A Little of both*

2. Did you feel wanted by your parents as a child? *Yes*

3. When did you first become a violator of the law? What was the violation?
Teens / speed tickets

4. Who influenced you the most to become a violator? *No one*

5. Do you consider yourself to be an inferior person because of your imprisonment?

6. What are the greatest stressors in prison? *Close living quaters*

7. What do you miss the most being confined? *Family, Freedom to move as desired.*

8. Do you see a mission purpose while you are in prison? *yes*

9. If so, what is your mission purpose? *Shewre Christ Jesus*

10. What contacts do you have with your family now? How often do you hear from them or see them? *yes, Once a month*

11. Has your family rejected you because of your imprisonment? *no*

12. Does your family encourage you now? *Yes*

13. What part does your religious faith play in your life now? When did it begin? *Day to day dependance, as a Child*

14. What was your dominate emotion?

In childhood *hurt / Disappointment*

In adolescence *happiness / Anger*

In adulthood *Disappointment / hope / happiness*

Fear anger hurt happiness hope disappointment

15. What is the most personally disturbing factor in prison? *You've have no privacy*

Macklyn W. Hubbell

1. Describe your growing up family. (functional/ dysfunctional) ⟍ Mother — Physically (Cruelly Abused)
Father — Alcoholic / Abusive to Mother
2. Did you feel wanted by your parents as a child? No. Step-Brother — sexually abused me
Mother was there but absent. Father never around.
3. When did you first become a violator of the law? What was the violation?
When I was 26 yrs old. Sexual Battery
4. Who influenced you the most to become a violator?
My Step-brother.
5. Do you consider yourself to be an inferior person because of your imprisonment? No.

6. What are the greatest stressors in prison? Heat, Overcrowded

7. What do you miss the most being confined? Spending time with nature. Fishing. Photography
of Nature scenes.
8. Do you see a mission purpose while you are in prison? Yes.

9. If so, what is your mission purpose? To see myself as I truly am and make the
choice to change from a hurt person who hurt people to a healed man to help
10. What contacts do you have with your family now? How often do you hear from them or see them? the hurting.
They have slowly drifted from me. No more Birthday cards, christmas cards or
11. Has your family rejected you because of your imprisonment? letters.
Yes ✓
12. Does your family encourage you now? No

13. What part does your religious faith play in your life now? When did it begin? ② October 21, 2012
① The Ghost shows me the err of my ways and day by day I
14. What was your dominate emotion am healing.

In childhood — fear, hate, anger, confused, suicidal, homicidal, lust
numb, hopeless, ↓   ↓   ↓   ↓   ↓   ↓
In adolescence — ↓   ↓   ↓   ↓   ↓   ↓   ↓

In adulthood — ↓   ↓   ↓   ↓   ↓   ↓   ↓

Fear anger hurt   happiness hope   disappointment

15. What is the most personally disturbing factor in prison? I have no more contact with
my only begotten Son: Michael Nathaniel Orrell, Jr.

Michael Orrell, Sr. #34572

P.S. I hope to recieve some Counseling
from you if you have time. I don't
trust Non-Christians

66

1. Describe your growing up family. (functional/ dysfunctional)
   — ANYONE U LIVED WITH = FAMILY

2. Did you feel <u>wanted</u> by your parents as a child?
   YES BY MY MOTHER, ABANDONED BY MY FATHER AT AGE 5.

3. When did you first become a violator of the law? What was the violation? 36 ... lusting that landed
   I BEGAN MOLESTING MY TEENAGE ADOPTED DAUGHTER, you in Prison?
   IN 2007, I TURNED MYSELF IN, W/O ANY WARRANTS, IN 2011.

4. Who influenced you the most to become a violator?
   — SELF, SINFUL NATURE
   — FATHER IS A CHILD MOLESTER. GRANDFATHER WAS VERY PROMISCUOUS SEXUALLY

5. Do you consider yourself to be an inferior person because of your imprisonment?
   NO

6. What are the greatest stressors in prison? MY ENVIRONMENT: THE FILTH, LACK OF PRIVACY,
   INTERNAL, EXTERNAL   DISRESPECT + LACK OF CONSIDERATION

7. What do you miss the most being confined? — ATTITUDE OF STAFF
   FAMILY, CHURCH, PRIVACY, FREEDOM, WORK

8. Do you see a mission purpose while you are in prison?
   YES, BY GOD'S SOVEREIGN GRACE

9. If so, what is your mission purpose?
   TO GLORIFY GOD + ENJOY HIM, AS I HELP BUILD HIS KINGDOM
   TO HELP PEOPLE RESOLVE LIFE'S PROBLEMS WITH GOD'S HELP + POWER

10. What contacts do you have with your family now? How often do you hear from them or see them?
    WIFE HAS CHOSEN FOR NOW TO HAVE NO CONTACT WITH ME, AND KEEPS OUR
    FIVE CHILDREN FROM CONTACTING ME. BUT MY BRO. + MUM WRITE ME REGULARLY.

11. Has your family rejected you because of your imprisonment?
    IMMEDIATE FAMILY, YES, FOR NOW, I AM HOPEFUL FOR CHG.

12. Does your family encourage you now?
    MY BRO. + MUM DO. NO CONTACT W OTHERS, EXCEPT FOR MY CHURCH

13. What part does your religious faith play in your life now? When did it begin? ELDERS + FRIENDS
    ITS NOW THE VERY FOUNDATION OF ALL MY HOPE IN LIFE.

14. What was your dominate emotion

   In childhood FRUSTRATION

   In adolescence HOPE

   In adulthood HAPPINESS → SELFISHNESS → HURT → NOW HOPE

   IE Fear anger hurt   happiness hope   disappointment

15. What is the most personally disturbing factor in prison? IE LACK OF PRIVACY, MDOC MGMT ATT,
    — LACK OF PERSONAL PRIVACY + RESPECT FM STAFF   ETZ
    — FRUSTRATION FROM NOT SEEING PEOPLE TAKE GOD SERIOUSLY

Macklyn W. Hubbell

1. Describe your growing up family. (functional/ dysfunctional) — *Father WWII Veteran*
Large Family — *Mother — No Divorce*
2. Did you feel wanted by your parents as a child? *Yes* — *1 Sister 1 Adopted Sister*

3. When did you first become a violator of the law? What was the violation?
Speeding Ticket
4. Who influenced you the most to become a violator? *Accidental killing* *44 yr billing*

5. Do you consider yourself to be an inferior person because of your imprisonment? *NO*

6. What are the greatest stressors in prison? *Corrupt Justice System*

7. What do you miss the most being confined? *Liberty Freedom*

8. Do you see a mission purpose while you are in prison? *Yes*

9. If so, what is your mission purpose? *Study & Work*

10. What contacts do you have with your family now? How often do you hear from them or see them?
Mother — letter - Sister letter
11. Has your family rejected you because of your imprisonment? *yes / No deploryou Reasons*

12. Does your family encourage you now? *Mother, 1 Sister*

13. What part does your religious faith play in your life now? When did it begin? *Very Young*
Controlling
14. What was your dominate emotion

   In childhood *Fear / happiness / anger*

   In adolescence *Hope / anger*

   In adulthood *Hope / anger*

Fear anger hurt happiness hope disappointment

15. What is the most personally disturbing factor in prison? *Pointed Review*
Wasted monies, Time, Governmental Spending —
People as employment Tokens; Badges of enslavement
Miss Froud by Government Agents — Police
Corrupt Judges - Prosecutors —
Federal complacency and compounding of Federal crime

Prisoners Are People

1. Describe your growing up family. (functional/ dysfunctional)

2. Did you feel wanted by your parents as a child? Mother Did / Father - Not so much.

3. When did you first become a violator of the law? What was the violation?
20 yrs old   Capital Murder

4. Who influenced you the most to become a violator? N/A

5. Do you consider yourself to be an inferior person because of your imprisonment? Yes,

6. What are the greatest stressors in prison? Lack of privacy + space/ Noise

7. What do you miss the most being confined? Family

8. Do you see a mission purpose while you are in prison? Yes

9. If so, what is your mission purpose? To help men rehabilitate themselve while here, with intentions of leading them to Christ.

10. What contacts do you have with your family now? How often do you hear from them or see them?
Mail - Mother, Father, Brothers   Dad - often (He's in prison too) Mom - not so often
Twice a year

11. Has your family rejected you because of your imprisonment? No.

12. Does your family encourage you now? Yes

13. What part does your religious faith play in your life now? When did it begin?
It is my guide and goal.   When I was 20 yrs old.

14. What was your dominate emotion

In childhood — happiness

In adolescence — lonliness / hurt

In adulthood — Lonliness / Fear / Hope

Fear anger hurt   happiness hope   disappointment   lonliness

15. What is the most personally disturbing factor in prison? Lack of privacy / Noise

69

1. Describe your growing up family. (functional) dysfunctional)

2. Did you feel wanted by your parents as a child? *Not by father, and maybe by mother*

3. When did you first become a violator of the law? What was the violation? *2005+/- Murder Charge*

4. Who influenced you the most to become a violator? *Nobody - my*

5. Do you consider yourself to be an inferior person because of your imprisonm~~ent~~ *~~No~~*

6. What are the greatest stressors in prison? *Other people & staff*

7. What do you miss the most being confined? *My daughter & wife*

8. Do you see a mission purpose while you are in prison? *Yes*

9. If so, what is your mission purpose? *To spread God's word, and help others.*

10. What contacts do you have with your family now? How often do you hear from them or see them? *Phone Calls and Visits / I hear from them every week.*

11. Has your family rejected you because of your imprisonment? *No*

12. Does your family encourage you now? *Yes*

13. What part does your religious faith play in your life now? When did it begin? *Major / It begin as a boy*

14. What was your dominate emotion

    In childhood *Very Aggressive, with much happiness*

    In adolescence *Very Aggressive, with happiness, and some disappointments*

    In adulthood *Very Aggressive, with Anger, Fear, Hurt, Happiness, great Hope, disappointments, and the list goes on, but God is still greater.*

Fear anger hurt   happiness hope disappointment

15. What is the most personally disturbing factor in prison? *Not being there for my daughter and Mother, and rest of family & friends.*

Prisoners Are People

1. Describe your growing up family. (functional/ dysfunctional) — functional   Born in 1974 —

2. Did you feel wanted by your parents as a child? Yes Very much so   2007 first offense

3. When did you first become a violator of the law? What was the violation?

4. Who influenced you the most to become a violator? Drugs + alcohol — America

5. Do you consider yourself to be an inferior person because of your imprisonment? No   Life w/o parol

6. What are the greatest stressors in prison? Anything can become a stressor... I don't stress much

7. What do you miss the most being confined? Snow skiing, scuba diving, motorcycles — corvettes pizza — ice cream

8. Do you see a mission purpose while you are in prison? — To serve Christ + love Him radically

9. If so, what is your mission purpose? To become more Christlike each day... to abide in Him... Trust + Obey

10. What contacts do you have with your family now? How often do you hear from them or see them? Good Contact   See them often

11. Has your family rejected you because of your imprisonment? No

12. Does your family encourage you now? Yes very much

13. What part does your religious faith play in your life now? When did it begin? I was saved in 2007 in county jail. I live only for Christ now. All day everyday.

14. What was your dominate emotion

happiness   — In childhood —

happiness   — In adolescence —

hope + happiness — In adulthood —

Fear anger hurt   happiness hope   disappointment

15. What is the most personally disturbing factor in prison?

❋ The closer I get to Christ, the more disgusting the sin + filth becomes that so permeates the lives of most men in this place. Very disturbing to see the evil ignorance that blinds so many.

1. Describe your growing up family. (functional/ dysfunctional) Functional

2. Did you feel wanted by your parents as a child? By my Mother ; I didn't Know My Father

3. When did you first become a violator of the law? What was the violation?
March, 2005, Sex Crime

4. Who influenced you the most to become a violator? Nobody

5. Do you consider yourself to be an inferior person because of your imprisonment? NO

6. What are the greatest stressors in prison? Not having Personal space

7. What do you miss the most being confined? Being with my Family

8. Do you see a mission purpose while you are in prison? Yes

9. If so, what is your mission purpose? To Do the will of God, by spreading His Word

10. What contacts do you have with your family now? How often do you hear from them or see them? I have A lot of contact
I hear from them often

11. Has your family rejected you because of your imprisonment? NO

12. Does your family encourage you now? Yes

13. What part does your religious faith play in your life now? When did it begin? It Play a major role in my every day life. August 2006

14. What was your dominate emotion

　　In childhood Happiness, love

　　In adolescence Anger, Distance

　　In adulthood Disappoinment, Violent

Fear anger hurt   happiness hope   disappointment

15. What is the most personally disturbing factor in prison? The fact that a lot of men are at their lowest and hurting , and the system as well as other inmate do the best they can to keep you down.

Chapter VI

Families of Origin

The family in our culture more often than not consists of an adult male and an adult female. Either through planning or through happenstance, conception takes place followed by nine months of incubation. Hopefully the end result is a healthy infant. In most cases in our culture, this process is repeated once or twice again, assuming single birth.

Obviously the embryo or fetus does not choose the male sperm or female egg forming a zygote. Of course, the same can be stated relating to the adult male and female. It all just happens. The bottom line is that nobody, neither the adults nor the newborn, has any biological input—under ordinary circumstances.

When the family of origin is formed, the family members, particularly the adults (husband-wife or father-mother) after making their genetic contributions, exercise influence over the newborn and the developing child. This influence can be totally negative if both parents are abnormal or have unacceptable moral and ethical patterns. In most familial units, parents make both negative and positive contributions, either minimal or maximal. And in the passing of time and with the adding births, the siblings contribute to the family of origin negatively or positively.

This reality leads an observer to ask: Who is responsible for the good or bad outcomes of the children? Father and mother? Mother alone? Siblings themselves? Any combination of the above? This reality leads one to conclude: All contribute to the emotional development of the offsprings. And a relevant final question to ask is: Is the child who develops into adulthood responsible himself/herself at least partially for his/her behavior and for actions –good, bad, or in between?

If answers to these questions cannot be made conclusively, it can be assumed, with a degree of certainty that the family of origin (individually or as a unit) had its input into the developing child or sibling.

Because of the acceptance of this assumption, I, as the professor, required that each incarcerated student describe his family of origin. Therefore, the twenty-five narratives, which follow, were written by the Parchman inmates themselves and later typed without any correction: The only alteration or change made at my directive to the typist was to delete names or any possible identification of the writers.

The following twenty-five stories of families of origin are their stories seen from their perspectives.

Person 1

The best place to start when discussing the success and failure of my family of origin would have to be with the head of the household. My father's story is a mixture of both failure and success, though not in that order. As a matter of fact, some of what I will contribute as successes of my father in the end turned out to be the very cause of his failures. I don't know much at all about my father's upbringing or childhood, so what will be addressed here is my father's life "as I knew it". The accounts will come directly from my childhood experiences and are not exhaustive. There may be successes and failures in my father's life that I am completely unaware of.

One of the successes I contribute to my father is the fact that he was consistent in the workplace. As far as I can recollect (which is about to age five) my father consistently held a job. Only once as a child can I ever recall "doing without" and it was only for a short period of time. Due to my young age I am unaware of the circumstances that caused this. But for the most part my father was a hard worker. There were two jobs in particular that my father excelled in. They were printing and painting. My father knew everything there is to know about printing machines – from how to run them to how to repair them. He has worked from one printing company to another for as long as I can remember. In between jobs at the printing company (as well as during) my father painted houses. He was a skilled painter and has painted houses for the rich on more than one occasion. For as long as I can remember my dad was a hard worker. He got up about five a.m. every single morning, save Sunday, and didn't come home until three thirty, or four p.m. I never once knew my dad to take a sick day.

Although I was greatly inspired by my father's diligence in the work place, it was because of this very reason that my dad came to one of his greatest failures. Because my dad worked from five to three I hardly ever got to spend time with him. By the time my father got home from work all he wanted to do was take a bath, eat super, drink a cold one and watch the game. By the time the game was over it was time to go to bed. My dad had to go to sleep early because he got up early each morning. There was never time to play catch or go hunting or just plain spend time together. There were occasional moments of fellowship, but they were few and far between. There wasn't much of a relationship between my father and I; that includes my brothers as well. My dad just didn't seem to have time for us. At first I just accepted this as one of the consequences of being poor: Dad <u>had</u> to work to make ends meet; and when he got home I felt he deserved to have some relaxing time to himself, doing what he enjoyed which was watching the game and throwing back a few Budweizers. Seeing as neither me nor my brothers liked football, (nor were we old enough to drink) we didn't spend much time with our dad when he got home. Only later did I learn that, regardless of what my dad <u>wanted</u> to do when he got home, he had a responsibility toward his boys. A responsibility as a father to raise up his children in the way they should go; to establish a bond with us by sacrificing his own desires and spending quality time with us.

Now, because my father neglected to do this, as well as neglecting to discipline us, both me and my brothers lack the example of a strong male role model, and we all ended up in prison. Every good quality that I have I received from my mother. This is probably the greatest failure my father made. He didn't raise his children as he should and he didn't leave a good example for us to follow. In the end, my father himself ended up committing a crime and landing himself a twenty-two year prison sentence. Day for day.

The most interesting person in my family would have to be my mother. She has a variety of successes that I will discuss, but she also some failures that can't be neglected to mention. The greatest success that I attribute to my mother is the way she raised me and my two brothers. My mother dileberately had my father move us to the other side of Meridian, away from his side of the family because my father's family were very racist. She did not want me or my brothers to be influenced by this attitude and become racist as well. She gave up a brick home with a big yard in return for a run-down trailer in a trailer-park. All so her boys wouldn't be racist. I am thankful for this action my mother took to this very day. In my opinion this was her greatest success.

Also, my mother (rather than my father) was responsible for most all of my "moral" learning. To this day I do not judge a person by the color of their skin – because my mother taught me not to. I address my elders, regardless of status, with the proper respect: "Yes M'am" and "Yes Sir", "Mr." So and So and "Ms." So and So – all because my mother taught me to. I may have made some wrong choices since then, but I am a gentleman to the ladies, a respecter of elders and authorities, a lover of animals, and know not to be wasteful along with a great many other virtues, all because my mother was successful in teaching me these things.

However, like my father, my mother's greatest failure is closely related to her greatest success. Although my momma raised my brothers and I up with good morals, these were simply the morals of a falling humanity. To be brought up in, and taught, the standards of the Holy Bible would have been much preferred. For no matter how good a person a child can be raised to be it is not the goodness of God nor the goodness he requires. A child of a "professing" Christian family should be raised up on the word of God and on the commands of Jesus as the standard of living. Because my mother did not do this she, for one, disobeyed God (which is a failure in itself), and left her boys to alter or decide to change the morals we were taught as we saw fit. This was not difficult seeing as both she and my father allowed a television in our home which, in turn, told me that I could change my moral standards however I wished.

The only other failure I can comfortably attribute to my mother is that she didn't follow her dreams. My mother went to college to be a professional secretary, but ended up being a homemaker. After me and my brothers left home she began to pursue her goal again, but never followed through. Eventually she and my father got a divorce and both remarried. Her new husband, Billy, gave my mother the life, freedom, and happiness that she apparently didn't receive from my father. Though her life contained more joy than before, my mother continued to hang on to some bad habits which has recently taken their toll on her. She has had two heart attacks because of cigarettes, but has quit the habit and appears to be seeking religion once more. All in all my mother's life can be patterned – success, failure, success.

Both of my brothers I cherish dearly, but I must admit that my heart has always been drawn toward my older brother rather than the younger. Timothy's life is a very good example of overcoming failure. Tim was the first of my siblings to do jail time. When I was 12 year's old Timothy got sentenced to five years in the county and 3 ½ years it was only me and my younger brother. During this time me and my younger brother grew closer together, but the gap between us and Timothy grew. Once Tim got out of prison it was only a year and a half before I got sentenced to life. Not enough time to renew the bond between me and Timothy. He eventually had a little boy and he named him after me. With a child now, Tim had to get a job – a difficult task for an ex-convict. He struggled with offshore jobs for a while, but somewhere along the line got hooked on crack cocaine along with my father. He then lost custody of his son and went through a difficult time of addition and rehab.

Tim was strong, however, and came through this darkness without returning to prison. He began to spend more time with his son and hold a stable job. It wasn't long, however, that he got laid off and work was scarce. In despair he resorted to the new drug on the streets known as "Spice". For the better part of a year he, along with my younger brother, became so hooked on spice that they were practically digging through dumpsters to find food and whatever else they could possibly sell to buy the drug. With the help of a female friend of his, Tim once again pulled through.

So far this was the last time Tim would fall in to a pattern of failure/success. The lady that helped Tim out of his slump done so by inviting him to church. Upon visiting this new fledgling church Timothy met the Lord Jesus and gave his life to him. In doing so, Timothy was radically changed. He quit smoking, drinking, and doing drugs. He found a stable job which he loves and has become a great father to his son. He carries his son with him to the same church and has begun to raise him up in the ways of the Lord. My older brother began a failure and ended up a success.

Joshua's story is one of failure. Really it is a story of one failure after another. From a early age my brother Josh ran the streets and lived the life of a thug. Josh was always drawn to drugs, crime, violence, and gang activity. He didn't do his first prison sentence until after I got my life sentence. He had been arrested many times before then, but most of them were only because of minor crimes. It wouldn't be long before the spiral downward would be a normality.

Josh started the gang activity when he was about ten or eleven. He began to listen to the gangsta rapper Tupac Shakur and desiring to be just like him. He would listen to rap music, smoke weed, and start fights. He took on the nickname "Smokey" after the character Chris Tucker played in the movie "Friday". All of Josh's role models were gangstas. After Timothy got locked up and me and Josh grew closer, I also began to listen to gangsta rap. Mainly because of Josh's influence. It wasn't long after this that Josh and I began to commit petty crimes, such as theft, together.

Once I got locked up Josh got married and had a little girl. A year or two later he and his wife got a divorce. Josh remarried and had a little boy. A year later another divorce, and a prison sentence of three years. After he served his sentence Josh got married a third time. Only this time the woman Josh married had a little money, parents who would give her more whenever she wanted it, and a bad addiction to pain killers and downers. Josh stayed with Kandi, who already had three boys of her own to raise, for a few years and became addicted to pills along with her.

It wasn't long before Josh and Kandi, who both couldn't hold a job, began to sell drugs in order to support themselves. Eventually this led to Josh's second prison sentence. He and Kandi stayed together during his incarceration, but divorced one another not long after his release. Josh resorted to little odd-end jobs here and there to support his new "Spice" habit. Josh had already burned so many bridges with my mother and the rest of the family that as far as I know he has nobody to turn to. From time to time Josh will be allowed to stay at my mother's house, but not for extended periods of time. Right now I do not know where he lives, but last I heard he was around some Christians and going to church.

Aside from this I can't think of a single success I can attribute to my younger brother. As of yet his life has simply been one of one failure after another and progressively getting worse. This is probably one of the most painful things I've ever had to do – bring into focus the fact that my younger brother is a failure. I trust in God, however, and I believe Josh's life will turn out for the best. He's only 30 years old.

As far as my family of origin is concerned there have probably been more failure than success. However, I am convinced that God doesn't measure failure and success the way we do. I know that no matter how much of a failure any of my family may be, God can transform their life in a moments time and flip the world upside down with their successes. I take my proof from the character Saul of Tarsus, who later became Paul, that what I say is true. Does not God always have the last say?

Person 2

Born April 22, 1958 in Holly Springs, Mississippi. To _____ and _____. The youngest of six children.

Lived in Holly Spring's for two years, then moved to the community of Thaxton in Pontotoc County Mississippi. Was raised there until the age of 21, then moved to the town of Pontotoc.

I attended Thaxton High School until the sixth grade. Two new county school's were built by joining the six county schools into North Pontotoc and South Pontotoc, therefore resulting one city school and two county schools. I attended North Pontotoc, starting in the seventh grade until the twelfth grade. I graduated high school in 1977.

I started working for Jesco construction company and did so for one year. The job required me to be out of town ten straight days off 4 days then back out of town. So I became employed by doing construction as a carpenter during warm weather and then working winter or cold months in furniture factories. I always like to work for myself, as to working for other companies. I prefer to answer only to the one I was doing the work for.

I got married April 22, 1979 to a wonderful woman named Lisa. We had one child named Korei. We remained married until November 1985.

After our divorce, I was a very distant person who became a very mean drunk.

I sought out rough bars that would always result into a hard night of drinking and fighting. I was always one who did everything exactly my way and would not conform to the way's of "normal" people. If there was something I wanted to do then I did it. I would not be concerned what happen in the end.

In 1987 I was convicted of homicide and was incarcerated until this writing some 28 years or so. My life in prison. My life consisted of working as a maintance man for 17 years an working as a camp support and going to school.

Person 3

This story starts with Yosef and his family in Berlin Germany. It's the 1920s and Germany had just been defeated in World War One. The country was in ruins and money was scarce. The future did not look like it held much promise for a young man with a growing family.

Yosef and Sarah had been married for some time at this point in history. They were both living in Berlin with Yosefs family which to my understanding was quite large.

Yosef worked with his father who was a trainer of thoroughbred race horses. if the stories are true, people from all over Europe brought their horse's to my great grand-father to be trained. But with war torn Germany struggling with the after effects of the Great War the racing community was going through some lean times itself. As a result there were few horse's to be trained.

Yosefs wife Sarah, my grandmother had been trained as a nurse. It was told that she worked as a private nurse for people from the upper-class. Even with this money coming in, it was said it wasn't enough. It was jointly decided that they should immigrate to the United States for a fresh start.

Once in the United States they settled in Chicago Ill. where there was a large contingent of fellow Germans. In fact a large section of North-West Chicago is still referred to as Germantown today.

Grandmother Sarah landed a job with the Capone family. Al, the head of the family took a liking to her from the start. When he found out that Yosef my grandfather trained horse's for the race track he asked if he could meet with him. Before the meeting, Al had my grandfathers history checked out through contacts in German.

After their meeting, Yosef was put in charge of the Capone stables located adjacent to the Belmont racetrack. Capones horse's started to consistently win races. Other's started to put their horses with Yosef in the hopes theirs too would win.

Yosef was quite successful with the horses. After a few years they bought a 160 acre farm in Aurora Ill. They raised and trained horses there for the rest of their lives.

My father Joseph was born and raised on that farm. He stayed there until he joined the U. S. Army right after Pearl Harbor. He met his future wife, my mother, while he was.

The family has it's roots in Landau Germany. It is located in South-West Germany near the French border.

The family immigrated to the United States just before the American Cival War. Like the Rabins they too settled in Chicago Ill.

The Schlesinger family had an Inn back in the Old country. When they came here they entered the food service industry. After a while they began their first restaurant. Thru stories I heard as a child I understood that it catered to the growing Jewish population of the city.

As the story was told in our family the first restaurant was lost in the Great Chicago Fire of 1871. When they rebuilt they had followed the Jewish population a few miles north to future town of Skokie Ill. Here is a fact that is interesting but unrelated to the story. In 1948 when Israel was pronounced as independent, there were more Jews living in Skokie than in Israel. I'd say that is a good customer base!

The second restaurant was a huge success. It grew over the years until it came to seat 250 people at one time. I remember being there as a child and it always seemed to be packed.

My grandfather, Walter, inherited the restaurant from his father when he passed away. The restaurant seemed to be the center of life for the Schlesinoer family. I was bought up in Granpa Walters household. During the day if the children were not in school we were at the restaurant, it seemed at times that it was our second home.

At the outbreak of World War II there was a shortage of qualified instructors in the Armed Forces. My mother possessed then a Black Belt in judo. It is a form of Japanese self defense fighting. My mother was enticed to enlist in the Army as a hand to hand self defense combat instructor. She never weighed more than 120 pounds her whole life.

My father's outfit was preparing to go overseas. They needed training in hand to hand combat. The unit was scheduled for instruction and they reported to the training area where they discover this small young pretty girl waiting for them.

Like young men through-out the ages these fellows could not accept the idea that this little lady was going to be able to show them anything about fighting. The hoots and jeers started with my father being the loudest of the bunch. One must remember my father grew up on a farm and like most farm raised boys he was pretty big.

My mother challenged anyone of them into the training ring with her. She said if any one of them could put her down they would be excused from the rest of the class. Well sometimes my dad isn't the brightest bulb in the package, he took her up on it. (What a dummy!)

She, as the story is told, literly kicked his hindend all over the ring. My dad wouldn't stay down, so my mom repeatedly put him down. After it was over my dad had to spend 2 nights at the base hospital.

I've always wondered if it was love at first sight. With both his eyes swelled up I wondered as I was growing up how that could work, things children don't understand . . .

My dad went over to Europe with his unit. Once there he was assigned as General George Patton's personal driver. My dad drove General Patton all through the war and was there when the high command stopped Patton at the Rhine.

After the war my dad went back to the farm to train horses. But he wasn't happy so with the G. I. Bill. My dad enrolled in the University of Chicago where he studied engineering. He graduated and entered the residential construction field.

My mom after the war also enrolled at the University of Chicago where she majored in Business. As you might guess, upon graduation she entered the hotel/food service sector.

While they were both attending the same school at the same time, they got together. One thing led to another as it happens with young people and they decided to get married. They got married in 1948 and started our family. In 1956 after producing 3 children, my parents divorced. We the children, were never told why they did. But it had to been something pretty serious for I never remember my parents being in the same building at the same time ever again.

We the children went to live with my grandparents on my mothers side. My parents, each in their own apartments, continued to be involved in our lives.

My mother came to work for my grandfather in his restaurant. Later, she decided to join the "Diamond Corp". She climbed the corporate ladder very quickly. In 1964 the corp offered her a job as a hotel manager at their premier 280 room hotel in N.Y.C. She took me and I moved to New York with her.

My mother tried to be a mother to us, but as I look back on it, I really don't think she knew how to accomplish that. For instance I remember in 1960 she decided that she needed more face time with us so she took the kids on a 3 week camping trip by car to the Grand Canyon. Cars in those days were not equipped with air-conditioning, it was in July, hot hot hot. After several disasters, she decided it would be better to stay in air conditioned motels with swimming pools. The woman had some brains after all!

As stated earlier in 1964 I moved to N.Y.C. with my mom. This move split the family up permanently. We became out-casts from the family. All contact ceased between the two groups. I never got a birthday card, phone calls, letters from my siblings, nothing.

I at the time didn't understand the "why" of this course of action. Now I do, grandpa as the head of the family wanted my mother to take over the family business. She declined, a huge no-no in a Jewish family. The wound was never really healed.

When I was in my late 20s, I decided to contact my brother and sister, which I did. At first they were standoffish but over time they came around. I suspect it was my award winning smile that finally melted the ice. I stay in loose contact with them just so I know whats going on in their lives.

My brother Scott was a transportation analyst for one of the biggest trucking companies in the country. He passed away this past year (2014). I regret that I did not know him as adult, all those lost years for nothing.

I met Susanne, Scott's wife only once. She is a stock broker and impressed me as a very intense, goal oriented person. It was very evident to me that she was very much in love with my brother. For reasons unknown they never had children.

My sister, Francis, is a High School Principle in Rockford, Ill. I know her even less that I knew my brother. She is much the loner type. I tend to think she has had to many emotional hurts in life and this is her way of protecting herself. While my sister never married. I think she married her job instead. It is plain to see her students adore her and she is well regarded in her community.

Person 4

I was born in 1961. My parents reared me up on Mr. Bruce Jones Plantation. The farm was ten miles east of Belzoni, Mississippi. Growing up on a farm gave me a golden opportunity to learn about agriculture. I was the last child born in my family.

Both of my parents worked during my childhood years. Mother worked in the cotton fields. I can remember going to the cotton field with mother at the age of five. Every day, I pulled a cotton sack behind her as she handpicked cotton off cotton stalks to put in the sack. Sometimes, mother hand picked cotton off the cotton stalks and pulled the sack with me sitting on it. We called mother wonder woman because she always worked to help provide for the family.

Mr. Jones raised numerous farm crops and cattle for a living. Sometimes, we had to go through a gate connected to a cow pasture to get to a cotton field. I loved looking and laughing at those cows as they ran behind the truck inside the pasture.

My father had to work around cows if it was too wet to work in the field after a rain. I had my first experience of dealing with cows one Saturday morning. My father took me to work with him to help move some hay. He had to spread out some hay inside the barn. I walked around the barnyard with a frown on my face from looking at and smelling cow manure. Afterward, I never asked or wanted to go to work with father after a rain.

However, I loved going to work with father during harvest season. Father drove a cotton picker during harvest seasons. I enjoyed riding on the cotton picker with him every day.

My childhood lifestyle change when I became six years old. Mother enrolled me in school. I never liked going to school, especially during harvest seasons because I could only go to work with father on the weekend. Mother made me do house choirs or help work in the garden after school every day. I hated working in that garden, especially when I had to pick tomatoes. I never liked picking tomatoes because of the large tomatoe worms that would be sticking on the tomatoes. I played sick numerous times to keep from working in the garden.

Father stopped working for Mr. Jones to receive a better paying job with the Aycocks. I was seven years old when we moved on the Aycock's plantation. I liked our new home because we were closer to town, and there was a forest tower one mile from our house. The only bad thing that I experienced as a child was watching father let alcoholism destroy our family spiritually, physically, and mentally. Mother separated from father because he became an alcoholics.

I was ten years old when mother moved in with Mr. Clark. We became residents of Indianola, Mississippi. I was happy for mother because she was free from being verbally and physically abused by father. I quickly became upset because Mr. Clark stayed with his auntee. We all slept uncomfortable because the house had only three bedrooms. Many nights I slept on the floor so my two nieces could sleep in the bed. The only good thing that I liked about the house was it had a swing set behind the house. My brother and I would race to the swings to see who could swing the highest in the air or to leap the farest on the ground.

We stayed in Indianola for a month. Mother fussed at Mr. Clark for not having his own house to stay in. We moved back to Humphrey County because Mr. Clark got a job working on the Parker's Plantation. We moved in a house next to the farm's shop. Mother enrolled us back in school the next day. I was happy to see my old friends at school. I remembered telling my best friend Glen about the swing set that I enjoyed playing on every day. Glen and I always shared secrets with one another. I smoked my first cigarette with Glen in the school's bathroom.

` I was glad when school ended every day. I spent my evening helping Mr. Clark around the farm's shop. Hanging around the farm's shop with my step-father helped me to get my first paying job. The Parker's gave me a job loading the soil bean planter after school. I was twelve years old when I received my first pay check. I was paid twenty-five dollars for the first week.

I received my first spanking at the age of thirteen. Mother wanted me to do some chores after school one evening. I sneaked out the bedroom's window to go see if the Parkers wanted me to work. The shop's foreman let me pick up paper inside and outside the shop area. I should've obeyed my mother words. Mother reminded me of them later on that night. She came in the bedroom with a belt in her hand after I got in bed. I never sneaked away from the house again.

School was my main concern during my teenage years. I worked only on the weekends, especially if I had an assignment from school to do. Mr. Clark took us to church every Sunday morning. However, he would never stay at any of the church services.

My parents moved to Springfield, Illinois, when I was seventeen years old. We moved in a two bedroom apartment above a night club on the corner of Eleven and Cook. Mother allowed me to go to the night club from 8 p.m. to ten p.m. every Friday. My parents got tired of listening to the loud music coming from the night's club, so they moved a couple blocks down the street. I continued to go to the night club on the weekends. The night club became my favorite hangout on the weekend, especially after I met Tammy. Our relationship had just begun to get serious when my parents decided to move back to Mississippi because of the snow. Mr. Clark moved back on the Parker's Plantation. I was unhappy every day thinking about Tammy and the good times that we shared together at the night club. Finally, I told my parents that I was going back to Illinois to stay with Tammy. My mother begged me not to go. I worked two months to save enough money to get a bus ticket and to help Tammy pay other bills until I was able to get a job.

I was hired at the Hilton Hotel to do janitor's work two weeks after arriving their. Tammy was hired to be a waitress at the night club every Friday and Saturday evenings. She allowed the job to cause problems in our relation. She had an affair with the owner of the night club. Finally, I understood why love hurts. Once again, I wished that I had listen to the advice of mother. I left Tammy's apartment with my clothes in a garbage bag. Her putting me out of the apartment brought back memories of the time that mother made father leave the house for being intoxicated from drinking too much alcohol. However, unlike my father, I did nothing wrong. I felt so embarrassed and disappointed because I had to stay in a shelter for two weeks.

Every night that I stayed in the shelter, I thought about going back home to live with my parents. I called my parents to see how they were doing. Mother answered the telephone. She asked about Tammy and fussed at me for not calling to say hello every week. We talked on the phone for thirty minutes. Talking to mother gave me strength to be stronger in tough situations. I tried to talk to Tammy every time I went back to the club where she worked, but she would never sit down to talk while working. I stayed in Springfield, Illinois, for twenty-one years. I spented my time working and parting at night clubs on my days of work.

I lefted the state of Illinois and moved to Minneapolis, Minnesota. I started working for Aspen Temporary Service the first week after arriving there. They would send me to Nordic Track every day. My hard work and dedication to be at work every day open up a door for me to get hired full-time at Nordic Track. I thought about Tammy every day until Annie Bell became a part of my life. Annie Bell was the supervisor over the warehouse department at Nordic Track. We because best friends and lovers three months after I was hired. Our relationship lasted for four years.

Annie Bell did not drink any alcohol; however, she smoked marijuana from time to time. I stayed in contact with mother throughout my relationship with Annie Bell. Mother and her became best friends over the telephone. Mr. Clark became very ill in December of 2001. He died a week before Christmas. I took a leave of absence from my job to go to his funeral.

Mr. Clark and mother had been staying together for twenty-one years after I left home. I stayed with mother a week after the funeral to help around the house. I told mother that I was going to move back home so she would not be alone at night.

I rode the greyhouse bus back to Minneapolis. I didn't know how to tell Annie Bell the bad new about leaving her. Also, I couldn't stop thinking about mother staying along every day. The greyhound trip lasted two days. I called mother to check up on her before I left the bus terminal in St. Louis, Missouri.

Annie Bell picked me up at the bus terminal in Minneapolis. I waited until we got to the apartment before telling her about leaving Minnapolis. She told me to do what I thought was right about the situation. Afterward, we spented the rest of that evening talking about our feeling for one another.

I moved back home one week later. I went to work for Mr. John McGrew. Mr. McGrew was a catfish farmer. I couldn't stop thinking about Annie Bell. I would smoke marijuana and drink some nights to try to stop thinking about her. However, my feeling for her wouldn't stop ruminating in my mind.

I realized that smoking marijuana and getting intoxicated from drinking was not going to make me feel any better about the situation. Nevertheless, I continued to spent my time on certain nights at the night club. Things changed in my life when mother because very ill. She was diagnosed with breast cancer in 2005. Afterward, I spented my time every day helping at home.

Mother died in April of 2006. Afterward, I went on a drinking spree for one month. I never called Annie Bell to tell her the news about mother dying. Mother had a home health nurse name Vickie who came to visit her three days a week in her latter days.

Vickie and I became friends before mother died. The both of us continued to be friends after mother's funeral. Vickie would still stop by the house to check up on me after mother had died. Our relationship grew stronger every time she stop by the house. We became lovers and got marry in 2008. I stopped drinking after we got married.

I thought that I had overcome my drinking habits, because I never wanted or had a desire to drink for a month. However, Vickie's whole family were alcoholics. We had a cookout at the house one weekend. Vickie invited her whole family to the cook out. Her brother brought some wine to the cook out. He talked me into drinking a cup of wine. Afterward, that one cup of wine made me drink throughout the cookout.

Once again, I allowed alcoholism to take control of my life. Also, I became so addicted to wine, that I allowed it to cause problems in our marriage. I allowed my bad choices to deceive me and turned me into a murder. I murder my wife in 2009. I thought about how alcoholism controlled my father life. I had become like my father before he died. My actions and foolishness caused me to be convicted of capital murder. I was sentenced to serve life without parole and sented to Rankin County to be process to serve my time in prison.

I spented one month in Rankin County and was sented to Delta Correctional Facility in Greenwood, Mississippi. I spented my time going to GED school to get my high school diploma. Also, I enrolled in numerous Christian programs to gain a relation with God. I achieved my GED in December of 2011 before Delta Correctional Facility closed down in January of 2012. I also achieved numerous Christian's diploma for graduating from the Christian programs. I thanked God for it all. I was sented to Parchman, Mississippi in January of 2012 where I now resides. I enrolled in the F.B.I. program sponsor by the New Orleans Baptist Theological Seminary here at Parchman, Mississippi to get a social and bachelor degree in Christian doctrine to become a full time Chaplain IRA. Once again, I can't help but to thank God for another chance in life.

I was born to Ava and Robert. At sixteen years old, my mother gave birth to Michael Edwin. At eighteen years old, my father had his first child on November 13, 1968 at 4:23 a.m. in the Grenada County Hospital. I was now a resident of Grenada County Mississippi. My father was born in Tallahatchie County Mississippi and my mother was born in Laurel, Mississippi.

Life with an alcoholic father was one filled with domestic violence. At the age of five, my mother could not tolerate her husband anymore. So she packed all our clothes and my baby sister, Yvonna Diane, and was heading to tupelo to stay with my Uncle Thomas. Before we could reach our destination, my father kidnapped his son and daughter. Mother came back to our home in Grenada and managed to recover her children while her husband was sleeping after extreme intoxication. As we were traveling back to Tupelo, my father managed to catch up with us. He had awakened as mother cranked the car up, but mother was able to escape temporarily. Eventually, father ended up running us off the road and into a ditch, but the police ended up being involved this time. My mother was reunited with her children and the unwrecked car was given to my mother to take us safely to Tupelo where our stay was short lived.

We ended up moving to Amory, Mississippi. Mother met her new husband in Amory within the next year. He had three sons from a previous marriage and eventually they had a daughter together. My step-father introduced pornography into our home one day while mother was gone to grocery store. James allowed his oldest son, Gerald, to view the pornographic film. Gerald began molesting me and it eventually led into stronger sexual perversions. It reached a point where I became confused about my sexuality. Mother, after twenty odd years of marriage, filed for divorce. My step-father committed adultery with a first cousin of his. A lot of this incestuous sexual immorality was common throughout the family.

The damage, as a child, of sexual abuse became engrained and stained within my heart. I ran away from home three times, but no one came to hear or see my distress call. I began having sexual encounters with my step-brother's cousins both male and female. I eventually began to worship Baphomet. Baphomet is a false god of Baal: the god of lust. The symbol for Baphomet is the encircled five star pentagram with Baphomet inside the pentagram. Baphomet has the head of a goat. I was introduced to Black Sabbath. They are a heavy metal band whose lead singer is Ozzy Osbourne. They began in the early 70's. Ozzy Osbourne said he has been the Prince of Darkness since 1979. He is connected to the Church of Satan in California. Their symbol is the five star pentagram with Baphomet within it. Sharon Osbourne, Ozzy Osbourne's wife, is involved with the church of Satan. She has a show called, "The Talk". She is the one with the maroon hair.

I began molesting children at an early age. I masterbated a lot even at the age of seven. I ended up having sex with animals. When I was young I used to torture and kill animals. I was involved in homosexual behavior. When I was older, I had a lot of fornication affairs. I slept with other men's wives and I have slept with wives men. My confusion was deep. I hated Christians. I hated God, Jesus, the Holy Ghost and the Word of God. I hated myself and I hated others. I used to take a crap on the open Word of God. I used to urinate on the bible. I have burned the Holy Scriptures. I was an alcoholic. I tried to wash away what happened to me as a child and what I was doing with adults and children. It got to the point that I had a desire to murder a child or adult. To sacrifice them to Satan. Before sacrificing them I thought of raping, torturing, killing, sexual encounters post mortem, and eating these victims. I tried to stab a police office and was shot in the knee. Today, I have three screws in my right knee. A reminder how gracious and merciful God has been to me. My mother was cruel in her physical and mental abuse as a child. I feared her. She terrified and horrified me. I ended up terrifying and horrifying others. I used to read my personal copy of the Satanic bible. My life was one of sexual violence and physical violence. God kept me from killing anyone. He saved others and myself from becoming a serial killer. I was a sorcerer of the Pharoahs. I had demonstrated unholy power unto some people who believed in fear of what I had performed before their very eyes. My faith in Lucifer was strong.

God has brought me through so many experiences in life that could have meant the end of my life. I turned upside down, in a truck, off a bridge into the cold November water. I passed out from hypothermia but lived. I hit a drainage culbert at ninety-five miles an hour and escaped from a Ford Fiesta with only a jammed thumb. God graciously let me live after a suicidal overdose on speed. My heart rate jumped to two-hundred and eighty seven beats per minutes. Thirteen more heartbeats and I would have died. I was born on the thirteenth and was thirteen beats away from death.

My life was filled with other narrow escapes and dangers, but that will be for a book about my life. My own personal auto-biography will come to life, one day. I deserve to be incarcerated. This time it has awakened me from my sleep. God graciously and mercifully kept me from dying to only then die again in Hell and eventually the Lake of Fire. I am not ready to leave prison, but that is only the truth. When God sees that I am ready, He will open these gates as He did for Paul and Silas.

I needed prison to wake me up to the reality of all that God, Jesus, the Holy Ghost, and the Word of God has to offer. God has given me visions of my life to build up my faith in Him. He has shown me these wondrous blessings for His Kingdom. I will speak to the rock and not smack the rock as Moses did. Moses only stood outside the blessings of God and saw them with his eyes when he could have stood inside the blessings where he could have touched, tasted, and glorified God with God's children inside the blessing because of obedience. Moses loved God and God loved Moses, but look what disobedience got Moses. Looked what it cost me to run from God, but only to run to God after dark, dark years.

As a child older women liked to kiss on my face jaws and hug on me all the time. I believe that had an impact on my life. Because at fifteen I had my first sexual encounter with an older woman that changed my life. That one experience took me to places in my life that I didn't think exist. Around that time I was experimenting with smoking cigarettes and a little weed. With all this going on my grades in school were dropping, my attendance and will to learn also decreased. At sixteen I was kicked out of school for auto-theft, the burglarizing of a vehicle on school campus. In June of 1996 I went to a training school, (displinary school) in Hattiesburg for 6 months to try and help with my behavior. I stayed there but at the last month got kicked out. They allowed me to graduate but told me at that time I must live the campus. During that time I studied to get my GED.

Ages 17-19 I pretty much worked and continued to live a riotous life. By that time I was experiencing with more drugs: such as cocaine, pills plus the weed, & drinking I was already doing. During those years I had a car accident that nearly killed me. Had been drinking all night and decided to go to my girl house in another county and had an accident. I went the sleep and flip the car about 5 to 6 times and hit a tree. I lived but also had to go to jail for DUI. I happened to get a DUI in 1998, 1999, & 2000.

However, in 2000 because of my behavior I incurred a 3 year prison sentence that led to my incarceration. During that year also I had a little girl. February of that year she was born and then in August I was led away to prison. I served a year and was released. After my release I still didn't straighten up. I still got in trouble, running from the police and doing crazy stuff. In 2004 I caught the charges that led me to prison this time. During that time of being in County jail and getting out I gave my life to Christ. I stayed out for about a year from 2005 to 2006. During that time out God bless me to bet a job working on the Mississippi River. In 2004 me and girlfriend had a son and in 2004 had a little girl. I worked on the River up until my incarceration. I loved working on the River because I was able to make money to get my licsense back and come out of debt. After, receiving my sentence I came to prison and while here I have accomplished a lot of things. I received my GED and other certificates. I am currently in NOBTS seeking to obtain a Bachelor's degree in Christian Ministry. God has been good to me to allow me to do this what I'm doing. I'm serving the Lord and looking for Him one day to deliver me from this prison.

I was born in Jackson, MS in 1974. I consider myself highly blessed by the Lord to have been born into such a wonderful family. My father's name is George G., Jr., my mother's name is Robbie. The best part of my life whole life were my mother's parents, William and Anna Rae. Every good thing in my life came from that side of the family. (I say that knowing that every good gift comes from God.)

My father was a self-employed business man. He owned a company called Un-Common Carrier, which designed & manufactured fiberglass bodies for delivery trucks. Both my grandfathers were self-employed business owners. Mr. Lloyd was in the oil business, was very successful, and truly one of the greatest, most loving Christian men anyone could meet. He loved the Lord and everyone knew it, and God blessed he and his family greatly.

My other grandfather, George, Sr., was in the carpet & oriental rug business. I followed in the family tradition and was a small business owner for about seven years before coming to prison for life. I owned and operated a very successful used car dealership from the age of twenty-five to thirty-three.

I know that many would say that they have the greatest mom on the planet, but mine really is! She is truly a very interesting and unique woman. Mother received her master's in English from Milsaps College in Jackson, she is truly on of the most talented and creative people I know. She is a very talented ballroom dance instructor/competitor, as well as a brilliant choreographer, having worked in the entertainment industry for many decades.

My parents divorced when I was about thirteen years old. Dad moved to California for about ten years and started a corporation called Verilux Motor Corp. that designed and built highly power and compact electric motors for automobiles, motorcycles, etc. my dad was a good man, but had a great deal of stress related to business finances and such which led to a great deal of frustration and anger which he unfortunately directed toward myself and my sweet mother. I spent most of the first thirteen years I can remember just trying not to make my dad mad in fear of physical punishment.

There were times when he went overboard and became overly physically abusive to me, this was one of the many factors that led my mother to divorce him. As I recall I was delighted for the most part when he moved to L.A. because at thirteen I was freed from a father's discipline who had no problem controlling and manipulating my mother. Hence began two decades of decadent adrenaline guzzling adventure around the planet we call earth.

All the negative aside, my dad instilled many great qualities in me during the first twenty years of my life including a strong work ethic, morals, values, discipline, dedication, and many other qualities that helped me grow into the man I am today. My father was an avid adventurer and world traveler. I grew up racing motorcycles, mountain climbing, snow skiing, water skiing, white water rafting, scuba diving, safari expeditions, just to scratch the surface. Thanks to dad I worked hard and played hard all my life.

During the two decades after my parents divorced, my mother's father assumed the fathering role in my life, and I am deeply indebted to him for all his loving kindness, provision over and beyond, and the wisdom and strong Christian morals & values he instilled in me. Most of all, I am thankful to my loving Heavenly Father for blessing me with a grandfather like him. My grandmother on my mother's side was a wonderful blessing from God as well. She cared for my little sister and I all her seventy someodd years as if we were her own children.

All of the true love and blessings I've known my entire came from my mother's side of the family. My father's side of the family were a completely different story. My mother had only one sister who had no children, so my little sister, Shelby, who was five years younger that I, and I were the only grandchildren. My father though had many brothers and sisters which produced many grandchildren on that side.

The most we ever saw them was at Christmas or Thanksgiving and maybe a birthday. I really cannot contribute positive attribute of my life to coming from my father's side of the family. They were a bit weird to say the least. But thanks to my mother and her parents, my little sister and I received the best of everything in life from college educations and beyond. My mother and her parents supported me and allowed me and equipped me financially to pursue all my hopes and dreams in life.

I attended Belhaven College where I studied business and after I worked in several very fulfilling lines of work before owning and operating my own successful used car dealership for seven years prior to my incarceration. I lived a great life those first thirty-three years from a secular perspective, living the American dream to the fullest. I made lots of money, had all the biggest fastest shiny toys a man could desire, all the prettiest girls, you name it. But I didn't have Christ, and that led to a path of destruction that would scar the lives of all my loved ones and many others forever.

I was raised in church by loving Christian family, but I was a total product of the false gospel of the west and my life was shortly destroyed by sin. At thirty-three I came to prison for murder having received life without parole. It took me losing everything to truly look to Christ for salvation. But now I have been born again for seven years and in spite of all the disaster my life has been made glorious through Christ.

My family did all the right things for me growing up, except really sit me down and insist that I know that Christ was my only hope. They never painted the true picture of eternity and the consequences of sin.

My family's history is pretty vague to me. My earliest memory of my existence is of me and my sister, a year younger than me, being in a foster home. I didn't find out the reason we were in foster care until I was old enough to understand. My mother was thirteen years old when she became pregnant with me and my father was almost twenty or twenty-one. For some reason my mother's mother didn't buck against my mother being involved in a relationship with an adult. My grandmother's approval of this relationship still puzzels me to this day. After my mother and father started a relationship, I was born and then my sister a year later. From what my mother has told me, my father was possessive and liked guns. He was very jealous and reckless at times and my mother, who was just a young teenager, this scared her. Though he was a great provider, my mother soon left him and I wouldn't meet him again physically until I was fifteen. I was almost two years old when my mother left him. Soon after that, my mother returned home to live with my grandmother and we depended on government checks to survive. My mother was young with no high school education and no direction into womanhood except for what she learned on her own. It was this lack of direction that ultimately led to me and my sister being taken from my mother and placed in foster care. I was two and my sister was one. Of course I wasn't old enough to remember the exact details but I've been told the story of how it happened. My mother had asked her youngest brother to babysit me and my sister while she went somewhere. I guess he watched us for a while and then he left us in the house by ourselves. Shortly after that I was told that I wandered out of the house and into the streets while my sister was in the house alone in her crib. I was seen by someone and the police were called. Once it was evident that we were left alone, the police took us with them and placed us in the custody of the Department of Human Services. My mother was about fourteen or fifteen when this happened. I remember me and my sister's stay in foster care in bits and pieces. We would get to visit our mother for only hours at a time and then had to go back to our foster parents once visitation was over. At the foster home we were there with other foster kids who we referred to as brothers and sisters. I'm at odds as to how being away from my mother at this time made me feel. I was still young. Not even five years old yet. One thing that was evident is how me and my sister stayed together as children when we were in the foster home. I was her guardian so to speak. Even at that age. Among the many memories that I have of being in foster care, the one that's relevant and the ultimate cause of us being returned to our mother is when I was sexually abused by one of the other foster kids who was older than me. I was about three or four when this happened and it was a major turning point in my life. I don't know how it affected my family, but I'm positive that this event and its effects have trickled down through the years and is the underlying cause of several issues I've had in my life. So shortly after an investigation and report was made of this incident my sister and I were returned home to our mother. When we got there, the first thing we noticed was that there was another child in our family. A baby boy. There was also another girl that was born before the baby boy, but she was with her father in Germany. We found out about her later, but we were too young to understand what all transpired with my mother and the man she had the child with. My mother was still young and didn't have the right guidance for herself or for the children she continued having. She eventually had six children. I remember us being poor as children and the first of the month was usually when we received our relief. This came by way of government checks and assistance. In our house, my mother didn't work and was in and out of relationships with my siblings fathers. These men from time to time would physically abuse my mother and the police would be called. The men would be taken to jail but my mother would always fall weak and take them back again. Since I was the oldest, most of the chores fell to me. I didn't always like this, but did it with pride to gain my mother's adoration. Due to my mother's lack of maturity, we would go without water, lights, and gas sometimes because of unpaid bills. We would have to use candles or borrow food until my mother was able to pay. I would wash my siblings clothes by hand and in the bathtub. I would dress them and put them to bed. All this I did because of the lack of stability in my mother's life. She only did what she was taught to do. She took care of us with what little knowledge she had. My mother has never been married, but my grandmother was married twice. Sexual abuse has been a generational thing in my family. My mother experienced this tragic sin as a child and so did my sister and myself. I think that this has been a major part of the reason my family has not been a success in my opinion. The lack of dealing with this sin the correct way each time they occurred dictated the actions of my mother, sister, and myself. I truly believe that had my mother not been molested as a child, she wouldn't have been susceptible to being seduced by an older man and impregnated at the age of thirteen. I also believe that if my mother had had a father physically in the house who truly exhibited Christian values, her life would not have been so tumultuous. The things she experienced and learned earlier on in childhood trickled down into the lives of all of her children. This is not her fault, but the decisions she made are. I can't point the finger at her and say because you did this or allowed this, my life is a complete mess. I can only help her deal with issues that are relevant today and try to change the direction her choices as well as her mother's and mine has sent us in. as I said, in my opinion, my family has not been a success, but the book is still being written. I thank God that He has given me the grace and sight to recognize the things that my family before me didn't and find correct ways to deal with issues that plague generations of families.

My childhood was very good. I had a loving family and we would always have family gatherings. During the first five to six years of my life I lived with my grandparents, not because my mother wasn't able or didn't want to take care of me, I just wanted to live with my grandmother, because she spoiled me and gave me whatever I wanted. Around the time I started school I went to live with my mother. School was a very serious matter in my life growing up. My mother and stepfather insisted on doing good in school. I was the only child. I didn't know my father. Then my baby sister was born and her father adopted me legally and gave me his last name. I did very well in school. I was very studious and I enjoyed school very much. As I grew older I had a talent for singing and my parents thought that's what I really wanted to do so they tried to be supportive of that dream in my life. As I said my childhood was very good, both my parents worked for the post office. We were very well off my sister and I didn't want for anything. I never really knew what it was to go without the basic needs of life.

As the time came for me to start Jr. High school everything was still going good. But around this time things also began to change. My parents were on bad terms and they eventually got a divorce. In Jr. High I was still doing well in school. Although I had given up on the singing I had decided to join the band sticking close to the music theme. Later on I started to act out. I began to get into trouble, and looking back I think I was just trying to fit in with the crowd. Since we had moved to a different neighborhood that was different from the one I was use to. Later on I discovered sports and I quit the band and I got really good at sports. This began to develop a since of arrogance in me. I thought was better than those who didn't have what I had and couldn't play sports like I could. Later on in my 9th grade year I was suppose to be the man at my school. I had been there two years. All the old guys were gone and it was my time. Well my mother uprooted me and my sister again. Now I would have to start all over to establish myself. Now I'm at a new Jr. High School and nobody knows me as anything but another guy in the hallway. Things went very well for me at this new school much to my surprise.

Since I had a car, and a little money, I quickly transformed myself into the man again. I would pick the guys up, we would go buy alcohol and go to what ever party was going and get everybody into drinking. Eventually this drinking began to effect me playing sports and eventually I rebelled against my coaches and quit. Even with all this going on I still one spot of disciplene left. I was a member of the J.R.O.T.C. and I had great respect for my instructors. So I held on to J.R.O.T.C. and I became the Cadet Major in charge of the J.R.O.T.C. at my High School. So my whole focus turned to military service. I went through school doing very well in J.R.O.T.C. I won several drill competitions and even received the Presidential Physical Fitness award. As school came to a close, I decided to sign up for the military and I would leave right after graduation. Well right before graduation my world was turned upside downside. Two weeks before my graduation my grandmother died of a heart attacked. After this I really didn't care about any thing.

Now that Big Moma was gone, I didn't even want to attend my graduation. Eventually I was convinced to go and do it for her. After graduation, the very next day I left for the Army. Well the next chapter of my life begins.

When I got to the base for my training, I was made a Private 1st Class, and a squad leader, because I had 4 yrs high school J.R.O.T.C. Soon the hurt of my grandmother death begain to cause me to act out. While in basic training I was teaching guys how to march and I knew how because I did it all through high school. Well when it came time for us to march in formation some of the guys would mess up, and I thought they were doing this on purpose. So in the evening we would sit out back and shine our boots, I would jump on the guys and beat them up. After doing this a three or four times the Army decided to release me. I was given an uncharacterized discharge, because I was only there a few weeks.

When I returned home, I had a choice to make was going to work or go to college. Well I decided to try college. To make a long story short, I got to college and I was playing baseball on scholarship, but I really did care, all I wanted to do was drink and party. Baseball was last on the list right below school work. I would drink and gamble all day at school never going to class. Eventually I got kicked out. I spent the next 10 to 15 years of my life drinking and selling drugs and that was all I cared about was money, women, and partying. I never got in any trouble with the police until I was 35 years old and the State of Mississippi gave 20 years mandatory. The crimes I committed were very serious, but I don't feel comfortable talking about them.

Person 10

In 1966, I was born in Metarie, La. My mother and father took me from Louisiana to my new home in Greenville, MS. We moved quite neighborhood besides the Greenville Mall. We lived on a street named West Sudan, in a little red brick house with black shutters.

Greenville was a fun town. I had the opportunity to grow up with some good friends. I attended Greenville Washington School, where my dad was the principle and football coach. I had six really good friends and we would allways ride motorcycles together. Football was one of my favorite passed times, we had a little "Pee-Wee" football team that we all played on. My fondest memories of Greenville were: playing at Mattie Akin's Park, going to the Mall, eating at Hardee's and shopping with my mother at Fava's and TG&Y.

One time my friend Mike and I and some friends got together. We had a bon-fire at a soybean field by Mattie Akins and almost caused an out of control wildfire.

It was my sixth grade year and my dad was offered a better job. We moved from Greenville to a new house in Ridgeland. My dad was given a job at Madison Ridgeland Academy as the new Headmaster. I started the sixth grade and quickly made new friends. I started having trouble in school and my grades were not very good. My dad took me to Dr. Schallorn where I was diagnosed with A.D.D. I was put on Riddelon and my grades still were in the "C" range. I just couldn't make the grades.

I began to get older and started playing football. I had more than enough girlfriends. I could never get along with the guys, but the girls seemed to just love me. I would stay in and out of trouble, with school and girls and I always used to get punished for my grades.

When I turned 15 years old I got my driver's license. The day that I got my license my mother passed away due to cancer. I was very upset. My momma was my world.

After my mother's death I went on many drinking binges, running with bad girls and the wrong crowd. On one occasion I got drunk at Jackson Prep, during a special parade. I was caught by the band director of Jackson Prep and he turned me over to my dad. Well, my dad being the headmaster of Madison

Ridgeland Academy, was not going to be embarrassed by his son so he sent me to French Camp Academy my senior year. I was 18 years old and I was doing my best to hold on to my girlfriend back home and a girlfriend at school. My grades were still bad, but not as bad. At 19 years old I graduated.

Well school was over, I moved out of the house. I got a job at Lindseys Hardware and started college. My girlfriend, for 2 years, finally broke up with me. I majored in electronics and robotic engineering in college. My drinking had gotten incredibly worse. I finally ended up moving back home with my dad, and dating some very bad girls.

After college was over my noticed I had a bad drinking problem. I had hit rock bottom about three times and I was twenty three years old. Life was tough for me, so dad sent me to New Road Treatment Center in Mendenhall. I would be there for three months. I got out and stopped drinking and started going to A. A. meetings where I met my first and second wife's. I enjoyed AA. I also went to see a psychiatrist, Dr. Lundy, at North Jackson Mental health. I was around 24 years old. I was diagnosed as being manic/depressive with Addictive Personality Disorder and Borderline Psychotic. I was given Lithium and Zanex. I would go to the hospital and see Dr. Lundy about once a month.

Well, things didn't work. I quit taking the medicine. My first marriage failed after only eight months. I ended up marrying again, this time to a girl who had manic/depression like me. We had conflicts because she was on her medicine and I was off mine. I had many jobs, but I couldn't work well with others, I would get addicted to projects and not go to work. Sometimes I wouldn't get along with the boss or try to outdo them. I would, of course, get fired. I went thru many friends and jobs but, still without my medicine, things just didn't work out. I had been working with a fire equipment company and vent hood steam cleaning company for about 10 years on and off, so my Aunt Nette and Uncle Nolan decided to help put me in my own fire and cleaning business. B&R Fire Protection was opened in 2002. I quickly began to get many, many accounts. Within 2 years B&R had grown into almost a one hundred thousand dollar a year business, we had websites, nice equipment and roughly 147 accounts. I was struggling so bad. My addictive personality was getting read bad and some days I would be so hyper I couldn't remember what to do or what I had done.

The computer became my new addiction in 2003. I couldn't get away from the computer. I would play video games, download movies and music 24/7. I got into a bad habit of calling in sick to jobs I had to do. I would lie about how the steam cleaner was messed up so I could stay home and play on the computer. This was my new addiction. In 2004 I even tried going back to college at Hinds to take Electric Engineering. Nothing would stop my computer addiction.

By 2007 things were going great with B&R and we were making money. I was so addicted to the computer I was building them and always buying computer parts and continuously hacking programs. I became a 24/7 computer geek. I fully computerized my company and began to develop website after website, I made up my own presentations, videos and business cards and invoices. But as my company grew so did my addiction. It was everything I could do to keep myself from spending all my money on my addictions.

My addictive behavior cost me a good relationship with my wife and daughter. Computers took over all of my free time. Even work kept me from being a good husband and father.

May 3, 2010 was my last day as a human being by society's standards. I was arrested and brought to the county jail. This was the biggest let down and rock bottom I ever hit. I was brought to see the psychiatrist Dr. Russell at my request and it was determined my Lithium level was extremely low. I was put on 600 mg of Lithium and Prozac. For the first time in years my mind wasn't so racy. I could actually think. Time went on and after 18 months in the county jail I received my sentence, 25 years. My family was crushed, my daughter cried out, it was a sad day. This was my first time ever being arrested.

Since I have been locked up I have become a Christian, my dad and I talk a lot on the wall phone. My brother in law, the attorney, has given me new hope in the form of a ineffective assistance of counsel hearing in January. We are fighting for a new trial because of my bi-polar disorder. He brought me to seminary to learn more about Him.

It's 2014 now and I miss my family, my daughter and my life so bad. I hate prison. But I do love the Lord and I know that He will bring me home in his time.

Person 11

I was born on July 22, 1954. I was next to the last of six boys and one girl. My mother told me she had a lot of problems with my pregnancy. While in the hospital, she was in a semi-private room waiting for me to be born. She began to hemorrhage from her womb. Luckily there was another lady in the room with her also waiting to give birth. My mom could not call for help, but the other lady pushed the call button summoning help. The medical staff was able to get the bleeding under control, but ended up taking me by cesarean section.

After I was born, the doctors discovered I was born with polio in my right leg. The only way to do that was, I had to have contracted it while I was still in the womb. The only extremity that was severely affected, was my right leg with emphasis on my joints. It was also determined, I had a mild case in my other extremities, but nothing like my right leg.

I was in constant pain all the time which holds true even today. My mom said, I couldn't get any sleep because of the pain. The only thing they had for pain back then was aspirin. She had to take the aspirin, dissolve it in water, and then put it in milk, juice, or something other than water. If not, I would spit it out due to the horrible taste of the aspirin. She had to do this several times a day.

She knew the aspirin was not doing any good, because no matter what they did, I was still in pain. I could not wear shoes, so I either wore socks or went barefooted. I wore my first pair of shoes at the age of three. They were special orthopedic shoes, with a steel bar embedded in the soles, in which I had to sleep with. Then I had a second pair, also special made that had a brace built into the sole at the right shoe for support. I know these shoes must have cost my parents a lot of money – which I'm sure they probably did not have. But somehow they came up with.

In the meantime, questions kept haunting me regarding – why the family left me as well as the Catholic School and the church. I also had questions as to why I kept having horrible night-mares of demons who had the faces of Catholic Priest's I knew. I was finally able to have a sit down with my parents. With tears in their eyes, they revealed to me the sexual abuse I suffered at the hands of one Catholic Priest who died while I was still attending Catholic school. At first I was very angery with the Catholic Church. As I got older, I became angry with God and even cursed and eventually learned to hate Him. I was also abused by two family friends.

I immersed myself in music which was the only means I had for happiness. Unfortunately, due to my handi-cap, I became a victim to bullying. I was getting into fights all the time. Usually, I had a group of friends around me most of the time while at school. But, I had no-one with me when I was walking home from the drug store after buying candy and bubble gum. By the ninth grade, I did not need to wear the orthopedic shoes, but I still needed to wear the brace. A gang of four attacked me while I was taking a short-cut across the neighborhood park. They were able to wrestle me to the ground and beat me so severe, I had to be taken to the hospital. My head was swollen so bad, the Doctors had to put me in a coma to bring the swelling down. In the meantime, the Doctors convinced my parents, that even though I was in a coma I was still in pain with my Polio and they had a new pain killer – morphine. They started giving the drug through the I.V.

After three days they brought me out of the coma. Unfortunately, I was already addicted to the morphine. Finally, after spending the summer recouperating, I was well enough to start ninth grade year. I was drum-major for both my eighth and ninth grade years. After the beating, my family and friends never left me alone again. I became very depressed and attempted suicide because of the beating, Polio, and the question of what did I do to deserve all this bad stuff happening to me.

I was found passed out in my bed barely breathing by my youngest brother. Somehow he knew something was wrong, and I was told later on he yelled for help. This was on a Saturday and both my parents was at home. They came running also to find me passed out. My dad attempted to wake me as my mom went to call our family Doctor, who lived two blocks from our house. The Doctor arrived just seconds later and came rushing to where I was.

In the mean-time my Dad found an empty fill bottle of pain killers. Between my Dad and the Doctor, they were finally able to wake me up. The Doctor gave me something to drink and within fifteen minutes I started vomiting. After what seemed like forever, I finally stopped vomiting. My mom cleaned me up and then it was time to talk.

With three of my brothers, my Mom and Dad, and the Doctor in the room, it was not time to find out what was wrong. My Mom and Dad was on either side of me both with tears in their eyes as well as my brothers, the Doctor and me. The Doctor finally asked me, "What happened that you want to end your life"? I told him how everything was just too much for me to handle and I felt the only way to make it all go away was for me to go away. My Mom and Dad hugged me and told me – that was not an option. No matter what they had to do to protect me, that's what they were going to. If any of us kids had any problems with anything, we can go to them.

With that, the Doctor checked me out one more time. He came to check on me every week for three months afterwards. We would talk for at least an hour, and he finally decided there was nothing more he could do. School started up again and a whole new world opened up for me. This was my sophomore year of high school. I don't mind saying I was a little anxious. After I settled in, things got better. I was now in the Big Band – the High School Band, and I couldn't be more proud, as was my family.

In my Junior year, I tried out for Drum-Major. To my surprise, I was selected to be the Drum-Major. Man – I couldn't be more proud. My family attended every event I participated in. in my senior year I was selected to be the student conductor at our final performance for the year. I was met by family, friends, and fellow students at an after concert party being congratulated. I could not hold back the tears.

In May, 1974, I graduated from High School with honors. My parents and I talked about college. My Dad and U. S. Senator were good friends. My Dad contacted his office and within a few minutes, the Senator called my Dad back. With the Senator's help, I was able to get the financial aid I need for four years of college. However, in August, 1974, my Dad passed away from a heart-attack. This tradgedy really devastated me and I was considering to not go to college.

My Mom sat me down, and told me, my Dad worked too hard to make it possible for me to get a college education. Quitting before I even got started was not an option – I did not have the right to disrespect my Dad. With that, I decided to go to college. After four long hard years, I graduated from college earning a Bachler's in Music Education, with a minor in Journalism.

I came back home and was appointed as the Band/Choir Director of the High School I graduated from. Even though I had a full plate, I went on to get my Doctorial in Music. Boy was that tuff! After four years of teaching, my best friends and I decided to join the Military. The President of the U. S. at that time signed an executive order making it possible for the handi-capped to join the Military in non-combat positions. My friend joined the Marines and I joined the Navy. With help from the same Senator that helped me get into college, he was able to get me an appointment to Officers Candidate School.

I went on to graduate at the top of my class with the rank of Commander. My first station was Pearl Harbour, HI. After six months, I was assigned to the Sixth Fleet out of Jacksonville, LA as the Executive Officer or the XO onboard the USS Saratoga – CVN 68. However, I had to spend three months at the Naval Air Station (NAS) in Pensacola, FL, abord the USS Lexington for training.

I served as Fleet Commander for four years, until I was severely injured on a rescue mission with Navy Seal Team Six. I was captured and tortured for three days until a rescue team found and rescued me. The enemy gave me shock treatment in which I still have nosebleeds. I have brain damage, in which my long and short term memory is effected. And the enemy took a sledge hammer to the very leg I have Polio in and completely shattered every bone in that leg.

I was taken to Washington and then Virginia where the Doctors performed seven operations on my leg to at least make it possible for me to somewhat walk. I spent my last tour of Duty as commanding officer at Arlington Cemetary. I received an Honorable Medical Discharge and released from the U. S. Navy.

I moved to Memphis, TN and lived and worked there for six years. There was another family tradgedy that occurred that put me in my second depressed state. This was an incident in which I had my second suicide attempt. My best friend in Memphis was able to stop the attempt seconds from me actually pulling the trigger. I spoke to my youngest brother over the phone and I decided to leave Memphis and move to Vicksburg, MS, where he and his family was living.

I went to work as the Assistant Director of the brand new E-911 Communications Center. I ended up having three major heart attacks and having to heart surgery. They put a stint in my heart and after one year, I was able to return to work full time.

I got married to the love of my life in 1993. We have three sons and give grandkids. We have been together for 21 years in December. However, while trying to be the good neighbor, I was arrested and convicted on the bullcrap I am incarcerated for now. A crime I did not commit. I have been through a life of total hell!!! Every day is a life or death day. I have already tried suicide twice – I have no problem with the old saying – three times is a charm!!! Wow – what a concept!!!

Person 12

My life isn't as attractive as others may be, but there are some things that we all experience that may differ from person to person. My mother had me at the age of thirteen or fourteen and we were relatively poor. We were on foodstamps the larger part of my childhood and stayed in government housing as well. I was the oldest out of six children. Three boys and three girls and only two sets of us shared the same biological father. When I was about one or two my mother left me and my baby sister with her younger brother. To her despair he left us in the house for a long period of time and I ended up walking out of the house and up the street with nothing but my Pamper on while my baby sister lay in the house in her own diaper unsupervised. Someone called the department of human services and me and my sister were taken from my mother and placed in foster care. We stayed in foster care for about three to four years and only saw our mother during supervised visits. During our stay with a foster family I was molested. I was about five years old I think and the woman in charge caught the incident in the act. I had to make a statement about what happened to the authorities and this incident eventually callused the department of human services to send me and my sister back into the home with our mother. By the time we moved back in with our mother she had had two more children. A girl and a boy. For the next few years my mother was under the scrutiny of DHS because they always had to see if she was capable of taking care of us. I hated the department of human services. I always associated them with the word separation. Life back at home with our mother was exciting, but full of drama. My mother always got with men who didn't know how to treat her. They would beat her and the police would be called. But a few days later the man would be back with my mother. Some nights I would be woke up by the sound of my mother screaming and crying for me to run and call the police. As I got older I became the leader of the house so to speak. When it came to cleaning the house and cooking sometimes I would be called on a lot. Especially when it came to keeping the younger children in line. I took pride in being able to do these things. When I was twelve I was sent to a behavioral mental health hospital because a few teachers at my elementary school thought that I needed it. I stayed there for three months. When it was time for me to leave there was no place for me to go so I was moved to a boys and girls club home. When it came time for me to leave the home I moved to California with him and his new wife because I had no one to take me in. my mother had moved without letting anyone know so my uncle had to take the place of my legal guardian. I stayed with him and his wife from the age of thirteen to age eighteen. I was kicked out by my uncle when I was in high school because of disciplinary reasons and I started working at a casino living life as I thought it was meant to be lived as an adult. Selling drugs, abusing them and drinking alcohol was a normal day for me. This way of life continued for me until I was twenty-one and ended up in prison with a life sentence for murder. Drugs and alcohol was ultimately the cause of my spiral downward.

Person 13

On April 9, 1957, I was born in Houma, Louisiana, my dad's native home. The city is located in Terrebonne Parish, inhabited by approximately thirty-thousand residents. The economy is mostly related to oilfield exploration/production as well as commercial fishing.

In 1960, my parents moved to Algiers, Louisiana, a suburb of New Orleans on the Westbank of the Mississippi River bordering Jefferson Parish. There, my mother purchased "Sal's Restaurant", and managed it's day-to-day operation. In the meantime, my dad pursued a career hauling freight cross-country via tractor-trailer.

My dad's parents and siblings were strong adherents of the Roman Catholic faith. In contrast, my mother's side of the family were staunch Southern Baptists. As a child, my sister and I attended Catholic Church and educated in the local Catholic school. When we visited our maternal grandparents and/or uncles/aunts in Hammond/Bogalusa we were invariably compelled to attend their respective Baptist church. Thus, I grew-up with a dose of both religious cultures and their indoctrinations. The theology of the two churches had, and still has, marked differences: one propagates tenets premised on Jesus' crucifixion while the other promotes Jesus' resurrection. These observations are, of course, made in hindsight.

Growing-up in New Orleans, or the "Crescent City", as locals refer to it, (Hollywood and outsiders call it "the Big Easy"), I was exposed to virtually every vice known to man. The City never sleeps. There is a nocturnal life as vibrant as those who work and roam during the day. As a kid, I had no difficulty distinguishing the difference between proper etiquette in an acceptable normal social setting as opposed to illicit behavior that could land me in trouble with authorities and place a social stigma on my family. Little did I know that this would, indeed, become a reality upon attaining early adulthood at age eighteen.

In 1975, I was offered a job in Bogalusa as an auto body technician. This mostly entailed repairing minor fender benders, often requiring application of a compound to fill-in imperfections, sanding, primer, and spraying on a new coat of paint. This was a vocation taught at my high school and one I truly enjoyed. My employer agreed to a salary of four dollars an hour plus time and a half for overtime. Business was good and often worked six days a week,

Monday through Saturday. I averaged sixty hours a week, entitling me to $280.00 minus federal/state taxes. Instead, my employer would always present me with a payroll check of $200.00, minus requisite deductions. Objections invariably resulted in an excuse that a bookkeeping error had been made by his wife.

On November 1, 1975, on a Saturday afternoon, my employer invited me to accompany him to Pearl River County, Mississippi on a squirrel hunting excursion. We purchased a case of beer because the day was unseasonably warm. The afternoon began uneventful, both of us barking squirrels from trees. However, there was a corollary affect to consumption of the alcohol and evaporation of our inhibitions. Hence, we inevitably had an argument about the more than nineteen hundred dollars he owed me. The argument became violent when he backhanded me across the mouth with sufficient force to knock me to the ground. As I got up he turned his back to me and began to walk away. Incensed, I shot him in the back with a .16 guage shotgun. He collapsed and died. Then, I compounded matters by robbing him of seven-hundred-fifty dollars, and returning to Louisiana. Thereafter, I traveled to Asheville, North Carolina, then came back south to Birmingham, Alabama. There, the FBI apprehended me via my 1973 Ford Mustang bearing a Sportsman's Paradise license plate.

The State of Mississippi immediately sought extradition to Pearl River County so I could answer an indictment for capital murder. At that time this criminal offense carried a penalty of execution by lethal (cyanide) gas. I waived extradition before a federal magistrate judge and was transported to the Forrest County Regional Jail in Hattiesburg, Mississippi. My attorneys investigated the crime, secured exculpatory evidence, and presented it to the District Attorney. Consequently, the capital murder indictment was quietly quashed, and the case returned to the Grand Jury, resulting in two new indictments: armed robbery and simple murder. On April 23, 1976 I entered pleas of guilty to both indicted offenses and was sentenced the same day to consecutive terms of 80 years (armed robbery), and life imprisonment (murder) in custody of the Mississippi State Penitentiary. On May 13, 1976 I was transported to Mississippi's (then) only prison facility.

In a sober state I was immensely remorseful for the life and property wrongfully taken. My attorneys recommended a jury trial, hoping for a lesser conviction of manslaughter. But I chose to accept responsibility and ultimately pleaded guilty without any bargaining or plea incentives.

Spiritually, I was an emotional wreck. In fact, for more than a decade after arriving at Parchman I did not believe God would forgive me. The first prison sermon I heard was in June 1976, a Billy Graham telecast on WABG, Channel

6. Dr. Graham exhorted John 3:16. repentence, and salvation. My mother and sister had sent me a Bible in the mail. I began reading Genesis, progressing to Cain murdering Abel. The story speaks of Abel's blood crying out to God from the ground, and Cain being punished by separation from his parents, homeland, and God. My guilt convinced me I was just like Cain and deserved to be incarcerated. I closed the Bible, placed it on a shelf in my locker, and didn't seek to read anymore scriptures for over ten years.

By statute I was required to serve a minimum of twenty (20) years before becoming eligible for parole consideration. My initial decade of imprisonment entailed conquering a tormenting conscience with drugs and alcohol to alleviate the recurring vision of my victim's blood crying out to God. This led me down a path of participating in virtually every destructive act imaginable within the walls of a prison. One of the first major illicit acts I committed was altering U. S. Postal money orders and posing as a unit counselor on a stolen telephone to facilitate cash money being sent to the prison concealed in a package. The enterprise was lucrative for everyone involved, except the unwary victim. The proceeds I accumulated were expended on other projects, such as drugs and alcohol. The latter became a necessity so I could get a peaceful night's sleep.

In 1986, I allowed a Volunteer Chaplain to counsel me. The initial meeting was at his behest, not mine. He was a knowledgeable scholar of the scriptures and had a self-effacing demeanor. Candidly, I explained that God's worth mandates a tooth for a tooth and an eye for an eye. Therefore, I reasoned, I deserve to die for taking a man's life. This was conveyed with anger. Nevertheless, he calmly replied, "Alger, I take it you don't believe God will forgive you." "That's right!" I said. He then challenged me to read First and Second Samuel over the following two weeks and allow him to come back and discuss those two books. I accepted the challenge.

Needless to say, First and Second Samuel primarily concerns David, a man after God's own heart. He was anointed three times before becoming King over all of Israel. Then he took Bathsheba, a married woman, committed adultery and impregnated her. He tried to cover-up his sin by ordering Joah to place Uriah in a position on the frontline for the purpose of having him struck down dead. The plan appeared to have worked. But, approximately one year later the Prophet Nathan confronted David about his egregious behavior and advised that God would not take his life. Under Jewish law, the adultery and conspiracy to commit murder were punishable by death.

Two weeks later the Volunteer Chaplain returned as promised. He had my full attention. I conceded that God forgave David. He then showed me where Jesus said that all sins are forgiven except blasphemy of the Holy Spirit.

Finally, he directed me to Psalm 51. David's lamentation to God became my own, and I was reconciled with my Heavenly Father and through the blood of Jesus was washed clean.

Today, I strive to share my testimony with others. God is a loving and forgiving Father. Jesus, too, emulated His Father by forgiving those who murdered Him. PRAISE BE TO THE FATHER, SON, AND HOLY SPIRIT!!

Person 14

Mack Jr., born May 26, 1963 to the parents of Mack Sr. and Corenia in Holmes County (Tchula) MS., graduated from Tchula Attendance Center in nineteen eighty two. The brother of six siblings, three girls and three boys. The youngest brother Kenneth passed away at the age of twenty six from a life long illness of poliomyelitis (Polio). Mack Senior passed in two thousand eight from cardiovascular problem.

Married to Bettie Mae in nineteen eighty seven, divorce in nineteen ninety one. One child, Syreda, by wife and three more out of wedlock. Deangelo, Romeo, and Juantaya. Two grand childrens, Brittan and Kaitlyn.

I have been staying in Mississippi all my life, working on farms with my father most of my life until I turn twenty eight. Worked at a mobile home facility for a few years until I got a job at Hunter Engineering Company as a painter at day, and took a trade up at Holmes Junior College in night classes, got a certificate and degree in welding. Continue working at Hunter until a major lay off in two thousand eight, which I call the year of crisis, and inflation.

Coming up in high school I feel in love with my ex-wife, Bettie. We met when I were a sophomore. Bettie was the love of my life all the way through school, and, until nineteen eighty seven everything turned sour after we got married. Nineteen ninety one things had gotten so bad and we were so angrily at one another. I ended up almost losing my life because Bettie was so angry at me that she shot me with a thirty eight revolver at close range in my chest. I was in the Methodist Hospital in Hinds County from February fifteen to April twenty third of nineteen ninety one. After that seems like my life have been going up and down hill like a see-saw. I have had my share of women after the experience I've had with my wife because I did not put any trust in women. So in between nineteen ninety two and nineteen ninety eight I ended up with three more childrens by three different women. At that time I was treating women like I didn't care about them at all. What I'm say is all I wanted was sex with no strings attached. And I really believed that they respected me for being honest with them about that. Even though most were married or had boyfriends in their life, but because I was honest, respectful and let them know how I felt of what I wanted and not them. It was all about me until I ran upon a young lady name Candice in August of nineteen ninety eight. I met that young lady at a funeral and I didn't no my life was about to change. First I was thinking that I was going to treat Candice like all the other women that I had had. Well I was wrong. It took me over three months to even have sexual intercourse with Candice. She had me doing things I hadn't even did for my ex-wife. She even excepted my kids as her own. The young lady changed my life and life style from having several women to having and being commited to her. After six years Candice and I were still together and I really loved this woman, so I proposed to her. And I was upsetted being turned down from marriage. Now that's when I should have cut all ties, but no, I still was with her. A couple months later she was pregnant and wanted an abortion. How stupid I was because she talk me into paying for an abortion and I agreed to do it. For some reason things were already bad between Candice and me, but when I lost my job in two thousand eight all hell broke loose between us because of a financially situation. Well, it was like a deja-vu, the same thing happen all over again after I put my trust in someone. I felt like I had been use, abused, taking advantage off, used physically and mentally.

I felt like I was push so far that it caused me to lose self-control, because Candice treated me so bad I wanted to take her life but I couldn't, because I loved her so much. So I commited murder on another man and assault on her. Now I'm suffering the consequences of what I did and also my family (mother, grandchildren, and children). My life tells me the expercing with women have giving me life in prison. Now I have to make the best out of life where I am in a celibacy state. When once I could have who ever I wanted. Now I look back in see the wrong I was doing. When I should have been loving and serving God.

Person 15

I was born in Independence, La. I was my parents' first child. I would later be joined by four brothers. I grew up in Ponchatoula, LA. That's where I went to school and church as well.

I can recall a very large portion of my childhood. My preschool years were spent mainly at my maternal grandparent's home during the day because both my parents worked full-time jobs. I can recall a time when my parents and I lived in low-income housing apartments. In fact, we moved to a house of our own when I was in the first grade.

The thing I most remember about my preschool years is that nearly all the kids my age had older brothers and/or sisters, but I did not. I can recall times when other kids would push me in order to provoke a fight. If I got the best of my opponent, an older brother would become his avenger. Such was life in the "projects".

I thoroughly enjoyed being at my grandparents' house during my preschool years. My grandparents were very kind people, and they were very good at letting me have my way. Granny always allowed me to enjoy sweet treats. Also, she would readily buy any toy that I desired. The best aspect of being at my grandparents' home was that I had a friend named Bryant who lived next door. Brian and I were the same age, and we got along very well. We were playmates our entire childhood.

I can recall the day I started headstart. I remember crying when my mother dropped me off there. I felt so afraid. I had an older cousin who taught there, so it wasn't too bad. However, I soon began playing with the other children and making new friends. Before long I anticipated going to headstart, playing with my friends.

I attended D. C. Reeves Elementary School from grades kindergarten through twelvth. Actually, kindergarten through fourth grade. I was a good student and made the honor roll each year. I rode the school bus to school and ate the school's lunch. I enjoyed those years of my life, but I remember getting many spankings related to my lack of diligence regarding schoolwork.

When I was is the fourth grade, we bought another house in Ponchatoula. This house was in the six-hundredth block of South First Street, one street over from my maternal grandparents' house in the six-hundredth block of

South Second Street. I liked the fact that I could walk from our house to my grandparents' house in less than two minutes. That made it easy for me to play with Bryant and some of the other boys who lived nearby. It seems that we all met up at Bryant's house because they had a large backyard and a basketball goal.

I attended Martha Vineyard Elementary School grades five through six. This time period was marked with trying to impress girls and being a class clown. I remember getting several paddlings at school for talking during class, chewing gum, etc. Yet, I made the honor roll from time to time. I did not particularly enjoy those years. It seems that a certain two boys and one girls always wanted to fight with me because I wasn't "cool".

I attended Perrin Jr. High School grades seven and eight. I enjoyed this period as I reached adolescence. I also was in the band. I played the trumpet. Since the band played at a few functions during the school year, I had a chance to get out of the house. I loved being in band.

I attended Ponchatoula High School grades nine through twelve. I graduated in nineteen eighty-seven. I didn't realize it then, but those were some of the best days of my life. I was in band, I played football, and I was in the Spanish Club. I did enough schoolwork to pass all classes, but my priority was socializing. I was very popular at school, especially my senior year. I dated and enjoyed life as best I could having strict parents.

My life at home was comfortable economically, but emotionally it was not. Life was so full of rules and regulations that made little sense to me. In retrospect, my parents were doing their best to keep my brothers and I on the straight and narrow. They did not leave room for error. They both worked very hard to provide us with a decent standard of living. They achieved that without question, on the othr hand, since they both worked (sometimes two jobs), I was not able to participate in most extracurricular activities because neither parent was available to escort me. What's worse is that the other children at school called me derogatory names such as "nerd", "geek", "momma's boy", because I could not go the places that most other kids my age went. However, things changed a bit my last two years at high school. Since I had a car, I could accomplish a lot more.

Within months of graduating from high school I joined the Army. I trained at Fort Leonard Woods, Missouri and Fort Belvoir, Virginia, then was stationed in Germany. The Army was not a bad way of life, either. There were challenges, pros and cons, but overall I loved it.

After a three-year enlistment in the Army, I went back home to Ponchatoula. I worked various jobs for the next seven years. I worked at a nursing home for senior citizens, a state school and two community homes for the mentally-retarded, and I also worked on the Mississippi River for Cargill grain elevators. Later, I worked as a Phlebotomist, a Lab assistant, and also as a home-health nurse.

I found that I truly enjoyed working. Like my parents, I often worked two jobs. I realized that I especially enjoyed helping those who had health care needs. In nineteen ninety-six I entered a "vocational nursing" program at San Jacinto Community College in Houston, TX. I graduated in August of nineteen ninety-seven. Shortly thereafter I was incarcerated and have been since that time.

Person 16

I was born in the city of Columbus, Mississippi on February 19, 1975. I am 40 years of age. My father's name is Darnell, and my mother's name is Mary. My father is approximately 3 years older than my mother, and according to her version of the facts, she and my father began to date when she was approximately 15 years of age. As a youth I saw first hand that my parents marriage was held together by many things other than love. My father was a man who could never keep a job. He either fist fought he co-workers or he fist fought his supervisors. He only worked well on jobs that required no supervision from others. These jobs included, but were not limited to, mowing lawns, moving furniture, and or fixing cars.

Dad had an overbearing personality. He wanted to lord over everything and everyone including his wife and child.

My father was also a very insecure man. I have either seen or heard him beat my mother nearly to death on several occasions: such beatings were over either perceived slights or some imaginary wrongs attributed to my mother.

He was a very jealous man – and mom could go nowhere without being drilled about who had spoken to her or tried to "holla" at her while she was away. Daddy was just a low down, dirty human being.

On the other hand, there was mama. An extremely strong woman, in fact, she was perhaps the strongest and kindest woman I've ever known. I have never missed a meal, never gone hungry, and never went without decent clothing while under my mothers roof. She stressed good grades. She stressed respect for others, especially my elders. She stressed cleanliness and reverence for God.

Mother taught me at a young age to do for self so that I wouldn't have to rely on a woman for anything. By age 9 or 10 I could cook my own meals, wash my own dishes and cloths. I could match and iron my school outfits as well as make my own bed. If left alone, I could clean up our entire house.

As I aged, I grew tired of the beatings and abuse dished out by my father. I had already attempted to kill him by pouring raid in his drink. (to no avail).

I began to run away from home in the fifth grade. At first, I would just leave the house as soon as I had the chance, however, soon thereafter I would just never go home from school.

By the time I finished the 7th grade, I had run away well over 30 times. I was sent to Training School and got out just in time to finish the 8th grade. That summer, having run away again, my mother came by my aunts house to inform me that she to was running away and about to leave town.

Mother advised me that I did not have to go, that if I chose to, I could stay in Columbus with my family and friends. To me, this was a no brainer. I could never let momma go anywhere and not be there to protect her. I knew that if I stayed momma would certainly come back. And I never, ever wanted her to go thru that living hell again.

My response was swift, "You know I'm going wherever you go, mama". From there we moved to a shelter in Vicksburg, MS. Mama later divorced my father and gave me a proper upbringing on her own.

I, too, married at a very young age. I probably around 20 years of age and, like my mother and father before me, my wife and I met at age 15. She was a beautiful, smart, kind and loving woman.

However, I was like my father in so many ways that it scares me. I was never really an abusive husband (physically), that is, but verbally. I was probably one of the worst. I cheated often, though not always guilty as charged. I turned to gambling, both as a means to supplement a meager military income, and as a form of stress relief. This later turned to a habit that spiraled out of control.

The gambling placed a burden on my family and our already tight budget. To compensate, I began to write bad checks, often leading to trouble in my military life. I began to rob any and everything – all while still in the military.

I would buy furniture for my house one day and keep the receipts, knowing that I would be taking something back for a refund within the next week or two.

My wife and I eventually separated, and soon thereafter, I lost my career as well as my freedom. Some would even say that I lost my mind, and to a certain extent, I agree. I don't know if my wife and I are still married. I do know that I miss her dearly and wish wholeheartedly that I could apologize to her.

I've been locked up for sixteen years and its been that long since I've heard from her.

Person 17

My family of origin begins with my great grandparents. _____ Sr. was my great grandfather's name, he was born in the late 1800's, he married my great grandmother in 1919 the late Sezzie Mae. In that union 12 children were born, my great grandmother was in her early 60's when she had her last child which happen to be twins. My grandparents lived a good ole life, they farmed their land and share cropped which was a way of life for black people back in those days. It was also common for families to be big so the kids could help with the chores.

Mr. & Mrs. _____ Sr. lived in rural Copiah County until they passed in the 1980's. They were always happy and proud of their family strict as well. I've often heard stories of how they were reared and it was no different from the way I was reared four generations later.

Mr. & Mrs. _____ Jr., my grandfather, was born July 16, 1921, he was the oldest of the 12. He grew up farming with his father until he started a family of his own. Big Pop met my grandmother when they were just kids and later married without dating. They were fifteen and seventeen, my grandmother was older. To that union 11 children were born. My grandfather farmed and raised cattle until his health failed back in 2007. My grandmother was sick and really taking a toll on him, but he stayed right by her until she died December 10, 2008. My grandmother Ruby was the midwife for the community for a long time, she learned from her mother in which I never had the opportunity to meet.

My grandfather's life continued on for several years after her death, but he wasn't the same. He and my grandmother had been together so long it was like part of him died as well. Big Pop suffered a stroke in 2011, and a massive heart attack January 31, 2013 and died, he was 92 ½ year old.

My father Mr. _____ III born March 24, 1951 the fifth child of eleven, he has ten brothers and sisters all are still alive accept one. Dad met my mother in the cotton field when they were very young, later they became boyfriend and girlfriend and dated until 1971 when they married. My mom and dad faced many diversities coming up missing school because the crops had to be harvested, and they were the first intergrated class of the seventies. By God's grace they were able to graduate and conquer the odds that were stacked in front of them. My mom has never had a job, she has always been a home maker. My dad on the other hand has always worked hard. And still does to this day. My parents have give kids and has never spent one night apart. Their kinda small compared to the one's they come from. My mother Sarah has 12 brothers and sisters, she is also the fifth born child. My mothers parents lived in Crystal Springs as well, her fathers name was _____ _____ Sr., her mothers name was _____ _____. Her father was also a farmer and a jack of all trades. Granny was a homemaker not much to tell. PaPa died at the age of 64, Granny died 22 years later at 86.

I am the second oldest child of five, I was born January 24, 1977. I graduated high school and attended a school of higher learning. I wasn't able to finish because of bad choices that I made. My childhood was okay. I mainly lived with my aunt and uncle in Jackson MS, but I finished school in Crystal Springs same as my parents. I enjoyed playing football, running track, and basketball. I received my first car at 15. My oldest brother gave it to me, then later on my dad bought me a new one. By the time I finished school I already one child and one on the way. He was born October 2, 1995 four months after my graduation. I attended JSU for one semester but I had to get a job to support my family. My father has been self employed every since the 80's so I started working for him, and later at the MS State Hospital at Whitfield until I turned 21 and got my CDL.

Living a life on the road is not for a married man. I married in the summer of 1996 and split up with my wife Sequoia the first 6 months on the road, two years later. To this union 3 children were born. Sequoia and I divorced some time later and I remarried had several more children, and started my own trucking business. I owned and operated six trucks, and later went to cosmetology school and opened my own beauty shop in Terry, MS. I became quite an inspiration to several people until I ended up in prison in 2009, seven years I've been here learning everyday to never return if they ever let me go.

Person 18

I was born on May 5th, 1961. I was named after Alan who was the first American to go into space on that day. I was born and raised in Greenville, MS. The Mississippi delta.

My mom and dad divorced when I was very young. I spent most of my childhood with my grandmother on my moms side of the family. The elementary school I attended was right across the street from her house. Her house was downtown on Central Street.

I can't remember how old I was when my mom remarried or how old I was when that marriage ended. I was lucky though, my stepdad was a good man. He took me fishing and hunting. We always remained friends.

In the fourth grade my mom moved me to another school so that I could go to my aunt and uncles house after school. My cousin, Susan, was a grade below me and we would walk home together. I was always close to my cousins, aunts and uncles. I had some really good ones.

Some time between elementary school and Jr. high school my grandmother got sick with what the doctors called hardening of the arteries. She had to be put in a nursing home. She knew enough to know she didn't like it there. I didn't like it either but I was to young to take care of her and nobody else seemed to have time to take care of her. I became angry with God then. I either didn't believe in Him or didn't want anything to do with a God who would let such a thing happen to my grandmother. She believed in God and Jesus. She had a nice Bible on the coffee table and a picture of Jesus on the wall. She used to talk to me about God all the time. I loved my grandmother so much. I would go see her in the nursing home all the time. I would cry like a baby when I walked out the door.

In the seventh grade I made new friends, started doing drugs, and skipping school. My new best friends name was Gary West. He was born with really messed up legs. It was hard for him to walk but he could get around. We stayed friends until the night he died in a car wreck. I rode to school with him every day until he died. When he died I quit school. I was in the eleventh. My mom and dad didn't like it but they just let me quit. My moms boss was the district attorney. He told me I was either going to go back to school or start jumping out of airplanes. He was also a company commander in the 20th Special Forces, C Company, MS Army National Guard. I decided to jump. I wasn't going back to school. He had a recruiter in his office and from that day on for the next 14 years 2 months and 18 days I was in the guard. I went to basic, A.I.T., and jump school at Fort Benning. When I went to Fort Bragg for S.F. school they wouldn't let me go through the course because I didn't have a high school education or a G.E.D. I came home, got a G.E.D. and ask to be sent back to Bragg. My unit wouldn't send me back. They wanted me to take sub-courses to get qualified. I didn't want that and transferred to a signal unit in my hometown. A good friend of mines uncle was in that unit. He was a like an uncle to me. I went with him to the MS National Guard Pistol Team tryouts for my first guard meeting with that unit. Nich was already on the team and trying to make it again. He wanted me to try out. I did. I made it. I also won the .22 new shooter trophy. I stayed on the team but transferred again to an aviation unit. I wanted to fly helicopters. They claimed I failed the first test by one point. I don't believe that. It was real hard to get a slot in flight school without knowing somebody. While at summer camp with that unit I met my future wife. We got married and shortly after we were married I went to crew chief school (helicopter repair) at Fort Eustis, VA. I moved to Hattiesburg where I had met my wife and got a job at Camp Shelby.

My six year enlistment in the guard was about to be up and my unit wanted me to reup. I didn't want to but my wife did. I didn't have to be in the guard to keep my job at Camp Shelby. She thought I should stay in because I already had 6 years done and it was an extra check. And you know how women like checks. Half of the state pistol team was Air National Guard. They knew I was thinking about getting out of the guard. I really liked those guys and they told me how much nicer the Air Guard was than the Army Guard. They said I should transfer over and get trained as a flight engineer or a loadmaster. I talked to my wife and told her if I stayed in the guard I was going to the air guard and would have to go back to school and would be flying a lot. She said that's good. Go for it. I did. I went to loadmaster school in Minn. Minnesota. While there the guys in my class and myself partied all the time. We stayed drunk. In short, that school cost me my marriage. I moved back to my hometown and started selling dope and being what we called in the air guard a guard bum. Since I didn't have a job (I quite Camp Shelby) I could fly any mission that needed manned! I got to fly a lot so I had checks from those trips coming in and I sold dope while not guard bumming. During that time I met a girl that was divorced and had a 2 year old son. Eventually I went to work for my uncle in Jackson where my air guard unit was. My girlfriend moved back to Jackson and then moved in with me. We lived together for 5 years. She went to Mississippi College and got a degree in nursing. Her son was like my son. He called dad. Not because anybody told him to. He just did.

I was activated for Desert Shield and Desert Storm. I hurt my back again and was taking a medical discharge. While going through the discharge she left me. She had got her degree, was making good money, and started cheating on me. Left me high and dry. I think its called reaping what you've sown.

Shortly after we broke up I ended up in prison for the rest of my life. I'm sour. Real sour. Sometimes mad at God. Always mad at myself. But I'll make it. I always have and I always will. With God's help that is. Only with God's help.

This has been a shallow look into the life and times of _____. It ain't pretty but its true.

Person 19

Success or failure of my family of origin and my marriages is the scope of this narrative, but how you decide what is success or failure is left open to interpretation. I will, however, attempt to reflect on some of my life's ups and downs, good times as well as bad times, and just see how things read.

My great-grandfather Edward, wanting something new for his life and the lives of his children, departed from Canada and came south to Alabama. Being a carpenter and enjoying working with wood, he secured a job with the International Paper Company. He worked there until his retirement. He was the father of my paternal grandmother Ruth.

Also seeking a new life, the parents of my great-grandmother Ida, departed from the New England states and came south to Alabama in a covered wagon. She became a school-marm and had an abundant amount of stories of adventures shared down through the generations.

Ida fell in love with and married a man named Wilford, who was only with her briefly. Owing to the pull of his rambling feet, he became a hobo, hopped a train and was never heard from again. Ida, being very lonely, was finally rescued from her sadness by Lee Sumner, the brother of Wilford. From this union came my paternal grandfather Lester.

Lester and Ruth, my grandparents, married. As a result my father Edward came to be.

My mother Mary's side of the family cannot be traced back as far successfully. I do know that my Paw-Paw Floyd was the son of a half-breed Cherokee Indian woman from Missouri. My grandmother Mary also came from the Ozark mountains of Missouri.

They were the owners of the Dixie Cab Company in Pascagoula, Mississippi until they departed this world in the early 80's. I remember staying numerous weekends with them spending countless hours riding in the taxis or sitting around the cab-stand learning to play poker from the drivers.

My Paw-Paw Floyd was a bit stand-offish to us most of the time. He was also an alcoholic and some say he was a Klansman. Because of poor circulation, he died of gangrene stemming from busting open his big toe.

From the marriage of Edward and Mary, my parents, came three boys, Eddie, Billy and course myself. Our home was filled with a lot of love and our parents were always there for us no matter what. I should have learned from them but somehow I didn't.

One of my fondest memories was after church the entire family would gather together for Sunday dinner at my great-grandfather's house. Grandparents, aunts, uncles and cousins all came together to share with one another the highlights of their week. Occasionally my great-grandmother Ida would make an appearance and, as the matriarch of the family, it was always a special time.

For the life of me I cannot remember what ended these gatherings. Whether it was the death of my great-grandfather, that of my great-grandmother, or just the way life changes. Regardless of the reason it was definitely the end of an era.

My grandparents, Ruth and Lester, had a very successful marriage and life seemed pretty good for them. I can only remember one time they argued and they brought up past failures to one another. It was more funny than anything, to see these two in a heated argument, mostly because they truly loved each other.

A major controversy arose between my parents and them over money loaned to my folks. It was a sore subject which caused a giant rift in their relationship for years.

I spent many weekends with them as a kid as well and that's where I learned about hard work and responsibility. They definitely shaped my work ethic.

My mother and father also had a great marriage for the most part. No history of divorce there, but like all couples they had ups and downs. Mom and dad argued once in a while and a few times this led to short separations. The longest was when I was a teenager. Mom and dad got into a spat and my father drew his hand back to slap my mother. This was a new one on me because he had never hit her before. I immediately sprang to her defense which resulted in Dad showing me, he was still the boss.

My mother took my brothers and I to my Paw-Paw Floyd's house where we stayed for numerous weeks. Eventually my mother and brothers returned to my father, but I opted of my two children, it was over. I could not forgive and forget; God knows I tried but was unsuccessful.

My father committed suicide in the mid 80's and it seemed he had been the glue which held our family together. I say this because it was the turning point in all of our relationships. My brothers went one way and I went another. We have tried to reconcile and even did to some degree for a while, but after I came to prison they made themselves scarce.

Mom moved to Alabama next to my grandmother Ruth for a few years but eventually moved back to Mississippi to be near her own family. She was in and out of my life and it seemed at times I only heard from her if she needed money. She did help take care of me when I was injured but later started drinking and got in pretty bad shape.

My brothers were the same way in our relationship. If they needed something then I hear from them. I allowed my oldest brother to move in with me after the break up of his marriage. He took me for granted though and did not respect me or my home and his free ride ended with he and I in a good old fashioned fist fight. I sent him packing.

My younger brother Bill was a wild teenager and started using drugs. One day he decided to hit my mother. It did not take long for one of my aunts to contact me and let me know what had occurred. I was able to get leave from the Navy for a few days and drove to Mississippi. Once arriving I had a man to man discussion with my brother which ended with him knocked out cold on the ground. In less than two weeks time I had beat up both of my brothers. Billy moved out of my mother's house and stayed with friends until he entered the Army.

My children, Bobby and Connie, were living with Jeanette. Being divorced and single again, I went on a rampage. I use drinking, partying, and sleeping around like a madman. I was on self-destruct mode and did not care who got hurt, including my own kids. At times I would pick them up for the weekend but after hanging with them for a little while, I'd find a sitter so I could go out on the town. The kids, of course, were neglected and suffered for it. They needed their dad, but I was too selfish to see it. It was all about me.

My children started cutting themselves. I am told kids do this for a release of anxiety. It was my fault. I was a weak man. They were in constant trouble as children in one way or another and their problems continue today, stemming from my neglect, I'm sure.

I remarried in the early 90's to a Texas cowgirl named Christina after only dating a few weeks. Our relationship started as purely sexual. We were "friends with benefits". Christina proposed to me and I agreed with no arguments.

A few weeks later she was sent to Alaska for a few months for her job. While she was away I continued to sleep around without a care in the world. I was a pig. Upon her return she decided she did not want to be married anymore. I was a little surprised but had grown cold hearted by that time. I figured she was probably cheating on me while she was away but didn't know for sure. We divorced after being married for only 4 months.

I again turned to the bars and the wild life. I was sleeping with married women, college girls, friends girlfriends. I partied, partied, and partied some more.

After a couple of months of living out of control and not being allowed to see my children, I moved to Mississippi to live with my mother who was really sick. She had suffered a stroke and was also hooked on pain killers and alcohol. I planned to only be with her for 90 days, but plans changed.

I met a girl named Margaret in a bar, my usual pickup spot and was smitten with her. We hit it off and dated only a short time before we shacked up together. We rented a house in Franklin Creek and lived there for a few years. I helped raise her two children, Anna and Brett. They were in need of a father and I needed them. Margaret and I were very much in love and our future looked bright.

Margaret and I bought property in Vancleave, Mississippi and also purchased a mobile home to live in. We were together for more than nine years living in a common-law situation. Her first husband beat and abused her and the children quite a lot which made her scared of getting remarried. We were engaged but she would never commit. I finally put her on the spot and insisted she set a date. She did, but we never followed through. I eventually grew discouraged with this situation and departed. I wanted to be married again and it was clearly not going to happen with Margaret.

I had custody of my son Bobby by then, he and I rented a cabin on the river. It was pretty wonderful for a while. We spent our days fishing or swimming after work and school. We also just hung out together and watched television in the evenings enjoying one anothers company. Dad and son, what could be better? Before long though I was need of female companionship, so back to the bars I went. This of course led me to drinking too much and again neglecting my son. He in turn began hanging out with the wrong crowd doing drugs and drinking also.

After a few months, I started seeing a girl from work, who happened to still be married. She and her husband were having problems and I guess I took advantage of the situation. We had been put in numerous group settings with other co-workers after hours and grew quite attached to one another. We had an affair without her husband or children ever discovering our indiscretion. Later Sherry got divorced after 10 years of marriage and two kids of her own.

I finally got to know her children and Sherry got to know my son. We would spend weekends together at either her home or mine. During the week, after the kids were asleep, I would come over for a few hours to spend time alone with her. This went on for about 8 months. On Christmas morning 2003 I proposed. We married on Valentine's Day 2004. I was in lust; she was in love; all was well, or so I thought.

After a couple of years of marriage I became bored and started cheating on her. Sherry had no idea. This went on for about four years. Following my arrest, she discovered my failings and filed for divorce. I tried to hold on to her, but it was not going to be possible. I was coming to prison and no way could I get her to stick it out, especially after what I had done.

My son Bobby joined the Army and was on his own. He got married at a young age and within a couple of months he got divorced also. He was still doing drugs and got himself kicked out of the Army. He wound up imprisoned in Texas on a robbery charge, but he was released after only 6 months.

After my son completed alcohol and drug rehab, he was released. He made his way to Jackson, Alabama to live with my neice. Subsequently he again made his way south and was again in trouble; this time for armed robbery of a few gas stations. He is now serving an 18 year sentence in MDOC.

My daughter Connie had remained with her mother in Virginia all the years. Jeanette, my ex-wife developed cancer and was dying. I attempted to make amends for the rotten life I had given or not given her, but I don't know if she ever forgave me. She passed from this world to the next on July 30, 2014. I did, however, get a chance to witness God's word to her before she departed.

Connie, my daughter, was left with too much on her plate and had a nervous breakdown. She spent some time in the hospital but continues to suffer from depression and personality disorders. She recently married a man I originally thought would be a good husband, but after only a few months, he turned out to be garbage. He decided he was still in love with an old girlfriend. He attempted to move her in with my daughter. This, of course, did not work, and my daughter divorced him.

Now Connie has latched on to a roommate they shared who is a drunk. Her life too is headed into the toilet. I set some great examples for my children. I continue to hold out hope for her.

My family's life has been filled with ups and downs, success and failures. I have caused a lot of turmoil and often I blame myself for the failures of my children as well. It seems as if Satan has sent his demons to destroy us. I have now turned my life over to Christ, and with His help, we may be able to salvage this mess before it gets any worse. It is not too late yet, we may have taken the wrong road and at times lost our way, but we truly do love one another, and God says, "Love conquers all." Time will tell.

My earliest recollections of my father's family occurred in 1950-51. This was when I was five or six years old. My paternal grandparents were both in their seventies then and lived about 100 miles away from us. On those occasions when we did have family get-togethers I can still picture in my mind my grandmother sitting at our old upright organ playing church hymns for the family to enjoy. Grandfather does not play an active role in my memories – he is just there. There would often be conversations among the grown-ups that I would be privy to that, at the time, just did not make a lot of sense to me. For instance, the "Copperheads": this, I discovered later in life, was not referring to a mildly poisonous snake, which inhabits North America, but, rather, was a group of people who were anti-Union during the Civil War and who actively supported the Confederacy even though they lived in the north. I recall that during my mental searching in the particular matter that ideas of copper bullets and other copper items were on my mind. Often these conversations at the get-togethers would focus on the life and times the early settlers to the region experienced during the time when Ohio was on the western frontier of the newly formed United States of America.

Then there were the _____ of the pre-Civil War era. This would be Elijah and his brother Owen. The brothers were active in the anti-slave issues of their day and both paid for their activist activities – Elijah with his life. I have not been able to decipher all that I had heard about Elijah and Owen as pertaining to how I might be related to them. The best I have been able to discern is that I am a descendant of one of Owen's children, which one I have no idea who they may be. Of one thing I am certain, my Lovejoy ancestor had to be a male, hence the name Lovejoy.

My grandfather, Samuel _____, died when I was in the second grade; that would be 1952. He had had a stroke and died rather quickly. I remember being there for the funeral and the burial in the family cemetery on the old homestead in northwest Ohio. My grandmother, Pearlie, also died of a stroke, this being in 1967. She had Parkinson's disease too, and I remember my father's letter to me saying that her death was merciful. At the time of her death, I was in the Navy onboard ship in the Far East.

My maternal grandparents, predominately my grandmother, were another matter altogether. The family begins on the Cherokee reservation in Arkansas in the very early 1800's when Sam Houston had taken a common-law wife among the Cherokee. This was several years before he moved back to Tennessee and become the governor, and later, a senator from Tennessee. Sam Houston would become enmeshed in matrimonial difficulties with his Caucasian wife in Tennessee and later immigrate to the Mexican territory of Texas in the 1820's. As things turned out, Sam Houston was instrumental in Texas winning its independence from Mexico and becoming a free and independent nation in 1836. Sam Houston was also instrumental in Texas becoming a state in 1845. Sam Houston did exact one concession of the United States Congress prior to Texas becoming a state: Texas retains the right to divide itself into as many as five states whenever it decides to do so. While Texas began as an independent nation, Sam Houston served as its president; and later, after Texas gained statehood, he served as Texas' first governor.

Frontier days in Texas were tumultuous. The Texans were adamant about ridding the state of any Indians (Native Amercians). Whole tribes of Indians were exterminated, such as the Karankawa. The Karankawa were very tall Indians, over seven feet, but very tractable and peaceful. Other tribes were either exterminated or relocated to other Indian reservations outside of Texas. The Comanche and the Comancheros were another matter: they were both intractable and very hostile. The Comanche chief, Quanah Parker, used two locations to live: the Palo Duro Canyon in the southern Texas panhandle, and the entire Indian Territory of Oklahoma – namely the areas around what are now Lawton, Oklahoma and the future site of the U. S. Army's Fort Sill. Quanah Parker would stage raids upon the frontier settlers from either of his hideout locations. Cynthia Parker, Quanah Parkers Caucasian mother, had been kept a slave for several years, repeatedly suffering the burning away of her nose by repeated live coals being placed on her nose and the flesh eventually being burned off her face. Cynthia Parker bore children, of which Quanah Parker was one of them.

Texas is famous for the cattle drives of the wild longhorn cattle that roamed freely on the Texas plains. Several cattle trails routed these cattle from Texas to the railroad terminus in Kansas. The Chisholm Trail was one of these trails and it ran through the western portion of Denton County before entering Oklahoma and going on into Kansas.

Not all of the frontier cowboys were upstanding citizens. One such group had stolen some horses from an ancestor's ranch and my great uncle Dan went after them. Great uncle Dan's problem was that he was alone when he caught up with them and confronted them. All said and done, great uncle Dan was lynched by the horse thieves in a large liveoak tree in the northwest corner of Dent County. My grandmother had me drive her to the tree when I was about twenty-one. She spent a couple of hours walking the area and, as is her custom, talking to herself – asking questions to which she supplied the answer that suited her best. I do this sometimes when I am perplexed about an issue.

The family ranch where my grandparents lived was large and had both beef cattle and dairy cattle. We also raised hay and some of the winter-feed for the cattle. The summer hay crops, there were usually three crops – sometimes four, were harvested during the warmer months and it was up to the teenage boys to bring in the hay. This was considered a "coming of age" point when young boys were put on the haying detail.

The kitchen table at the ranch house was always the center of activity. Many notable people say at my grandparent's kitchen table. I remember Sam Rayburn, Lyndon Johnson, and Audie Murphy being at the house. I was too young to know the importance of these personages to American politics or their contributions while in the military and I, due to being naïve about the matter, conducted myself among them when they were in our company as if they were family or close neighbors. I would also meet Mr. Dwight Eisenhower when he first campaigned for the presidency, I know that grandfather and Lyndon Johnson were old time ranchers who had grown up helping each other build and prosper their ranches – this was a very common neighborly act among them, even though they were separated by counties. In early Texas, distance or localities were designated in counties, not miles – there were just too many miles for figuring.

My grandfather died in 1962 as the result of a stroke. He had received a letter from ex-president Eisenhower only days before his death thanking him for his service in both World War I and World War II. Grandmother died in 1988, also of a stroke.

My father, Doyle, Sr., was born in Pioneer County, Ohio in 1916. He quit school in the fourth grade and went to work for the newly created airport in Detroit, Michigan, where he discovered his love of flying and anything aviation. During World War II, while serving with General Claire Chenault in China, my father completed his high school requirements in order to be admitted to aviation school as a glider pilot. My favorite memories of my father are when he would take my flying with him. Father was a highline electrician by trade and usually very distant and authoritarian – downright bullheaded. He was an alcoholic for many years and a womanizer; this being the cause of my parents divorce in 1958. My father died of a massive stroke in 1976 and I was able to return to the state in time for his burial; he was 59 years old at the time of his death.

My mother, Laura, was born in 1921 in Cove, Arkansas. She finished high school and attended college where she earned her First Class FCC License and worked at the local radio station, KDNT 1440 kHz in Denton, Texas, as the daytime engineer. She worked at the station until the end of World War II. After divorcing my father in 1958, my mother went back to college and earned her nursing degree at Baylor Medical School in Dallas. She worked for a group of obstetricians as a private duty nurse who would tend to all of their patients before calling the doctor who would arrive in time to help the mother deliver her baby. After I had been trained as a combat medic as my secondary skill in the military my mother tried to get me to apply for certification as a midwife in the state of Texas. My mother was very nurturing as well as my best friend and advisor. I was able to talk to her in 2003 just before she passed due to a stroke. I did not tell my mother good-bye; I simply said I would see her again in heaven. I have not grieved my mother's passing, as I know that God has things well in hand and He does not need any help from me to do His will.

Growing up I had two brothers and one sister. My sister is next behind me and I admit that we do not get along well together. As children, we were always at odds with each other and today we are still at odds with each other. My brothers, John and Bill, are two very different people. John, next in line, is very likable and outgoing. He and I often worked together and were able to accomplish many complicated and hazardous chores by working closely together. Brother Bill, an exact duplicate of our father, is also a testy proposition. Bill is hardheaded and authoritarian. While Bill may appear to be on your side in a matter, he is not to be trusted – he will turn on you in a heartbeat. Bill and I still correspond with each other, but our letters are infrequent and short – just the facts so that I may be advised of important family issues, such as births and deaths.

My family is another story of distance and "see ya later". My wife, Eunice Virginia, and I married in 1969 just prior to my last tour in Vietnam. "Ginger", my wife's given name, attended college in Mississippi. Ginger attended one year at Mississippi College and one year at the University of South Mississippi. Ginger was a decent enough wife but a sorry housekeeper. She doted on all of our children, having no detectable favorite. While lenient in disciplining the children, she was able to manage the household while I was away on deployments, often leaving the serious disciplining to me to handle upon my return home. Late discipline is better than no discipline, but I realized that late disciplining is when I would spend time with the errant child, talking to them and just being a father offering corrective advice. There were times when I used the belt, but that was only when I caught them in the act or they repeatedly disobeyed instructions from either my wife or I.

I had just arrived in Vietnam when I received a letter from a little white knitted bootee in it. Five weeks after returning to the states, my first son, Sam, was born and what a treasure he has been to me. Sam, as a young child, was a fast learner and has never met a stranger. Everyone we knew loved Sam. Sam was an excellent student at school whose only fault was when he would learn something his father did not comprehend, such as trigonometry, he would create a situation where I would be embarrassed. Sam joined the Navy after high school as a Quartermaster (navigator) and is knowledgeable enough of celestial navigation to pilot a U. S. Navy minesweeper over two-thousand miles and arrive within one-half mile of his intended destination. Sam is my only offspring to maintain contact with me during my prison experience.

Our next child, Robert Daniel, died in infancy, being only two days old when he died of Hyaline Membrane Disease. He is buried in Oakwood Park Cemetery in Scott County, Mississippi. My wife never recovered from the loss of this child. She continued to blame herself in spite of my best efforts to help her understand that sometimes we have no control over these matters and it is best for us to leave these things in the hands of our creator.

Following Daniel is Anne Marie, our only daughter. Anne is a very determined person who competes savagely with her brothers. At the dinner table, she had no problem with being a glutton like her brothers. In children's games, she competed actively with the boys and she probably was a tomboy. Anne was not a happy camper when puberty set in and her body began to change into that of a young woman. After high school, Anne enlisted in the U. S. Navy as a hospital corpsman. She completed her training at the Naval Hospital in Newport, Rhode Island. Later, she applied for and was accepted into the Nurse Practitioner program and she spent the next two years at Fort Sam Houston in San Antonio, Texas training as a nurse practitioner. Upon completion of two years training she transferred to the Balboa Naval Hospital, in San Diego, California where she is assigned to Seal Team Two. When a team deploys, she, in rotation with other NP's, deploy to the region with them. As a tomboy, Anne would shoot the guns just as her brothers did. When she was required to qualify on all military weapons up to .50-caliber machine gun, she tried to avoid the training. The Navy convinced her that it was in her best interest to qualify, which she did. Her marksmanship scores were in the top five percent of her class. Whatever Ann decides to do, she does it with all her heart and is very successful in all of her endeavors.

My son Pete, Virgil Webster, is the heavyweight of the children. Pete, as a child, was always content to play by himself. He liked trucks and construction equipment toys. Pete moved a five cubic yard pile of gravel from beside the garage out onto the driveway as he was instructed how to do by his father using only his "TONKA" trucks. Pete was always big for his age and as such became the protector of the family. I received a telephone call from the Pete's school principal one afternoon who requested that I come to the school and collect my unruly son. Upon arriving at the school, I was ushered into a meeting with the principal and another parent. Apparently, there had been a fight and Pete was blamed for starting the fight. The facts revealed that the other boy in the fight, a high school senior, had touched my daughter, Anne, inappropriately and Pete took issue about this. Pete did a thorough job of whipping the high school senior – Pete was in the sixth grade when this happened. Both boys were suspended for two weeks, so Pete and I went fishing – a just reward for holding up for his sister. Pete was in the U. S. Army as a Combat Medic with the Fourth Stryker Brigade in Iraq for one tour of duty. He is now a truck driver, a job he dearly loves.

Johnathan West is the child who adores both his father and his mother. He tries to imitate everything he sees his parents doing and the result is that he is a very devoted and capable parent. John-jon is the only one of my children to suffer as a casualty while in combat. He is the sole survivor of an improvised explosive device while serving at Forward Operating Base Sharana in Afghanistan. John-jon is still going through the agonies of PSD because to this event.

Lastly, there is Charlie, Charles Edward. Charlie is a carbon copy of Sam: bright, loveable, never met a stranger, and very conscientious of his actions. Charlie is in the U. S. Army National Guard as a quartermaster (storekeeper). Charlie learned to ride a bicycle before he was three years old and was able to read and write before he was four years old. When he wanted his share of the time on the family computer, he asked me to teach him how to type. I put a typing program on the computer, showed him how to use it, and away he went. By the time he was seven years old he could type over fifty words a minute.

In closing, all five of my children are war veterans – taking after their father's heritage, so says Sam. I am proud of each of them, realizing that each is his own person and must be treated that way. I regret that John-jon has not come to talk about his event in Afghanistan, but it is my hope that one day he will come to me and open up. I feel I can help him deal with these issues, having been there myself. The rest, well, time will tell. I feel that as long as I am locked up the children probably will not come to see me. I do not blame them; I would not want to see my father locked up either.

This is an account of the foundation of success and failure of my family. I was born on November 6, 1955 in Philadelphia, Pennsylvania to Joe and Barbara. Starting on my fathers side with the great grand-parents which are Walter who was a dariy farmer in Chester, South Carolina. He was married to Ruth who was a homemaker, and boy could she cook, especially pies and cakes. She was a Christian lady living her life for Christ. My great grand-father I am not sure if he knew Christ or not. He died in a car accident. I was five year old, when I first met them. Great grandmom Ruth lived up to 80's or 90's before she passed away. They had three children that I know of, and they stayed married throughout their life.

There was Henest who was named after my great grand-father had past away inherit the dariy farm taking on its responsibilities. He was married and had a son named Ronnie. His wife was also a homemaker which could cook while. She too cooked for all the hired hands for the farm. Even for relative who would show up at lunch. They never divorced and she out lived my Great Uncle Henest, as he passed away first. Ronnie their son graduated high school and went into the Air Force while he went to school to learn agriculture. He too inherit the dariy farm but change over to a cattle farm than back into a dariy farm. His wife is a homemaker and helps my cousin Ronnie's mother. They have two children a boy and girl. Than there is my Great Uncle Frank not sure what his occupation but he retired from it. In addition, him helping Ronnie with the farm. He is married to my Great Aunt Francis and they are still married. Great Uncle Frank like rodeo and horses. He had a rodeo on his land, and held them especially for family reunions. They had two girls who's names are Joice and Nancy. Joice is married to Buddy and they have three girls. My Great Aunt Francis and Joice are in partnership in a Daycare. Buddy works for a food product company. They are still married that I know of. Nancy is married and they both own a Sear's outlet. They have two children a boy and girl. Nancy and her husband are still married. Then there is my grand-parents Joe and Mattie May. My grand-father worked in a textile cotton mill and when he retire had his own convenience store. He died a horrifying death while having a heart attack. A ambalance came to take him to the hospital when the driver lost control going around a curve in the road. The back doors of the ambalance open, and he was force out still stripped to the gurney cutting him up which caused his death. This making my grand-mother a widow. Sure they had problems throughout their but they stuck it out through thick or thin.

My grandmother was also a homemaker. She never remarried. They had six children. Aunt Janet is married to Jessie and they have one child who's name is Kim. Do not know what Uncle Jessie's occupation is but Aunt Janet was a homemaker. They are still married. Aunt Patsy is married to Uncle Marion and they have three children. Uncle Marion works for the Natural Gas Company and Aunt Patsy is a homemaker. Then there is my Aunt Diana and she's married to Uncle Sisco. Uncle Sisco owns a convenience store which my Aunt Diana helps out too along with being a homemaker. They had two children but one died in a car accident the other is still alive. Uncle Sisco and Aunt Diana are still married. Uncle Wayne was never married but had two children out of wedlock. Their mother died in a car accident. Uncle Dean is the youngest of all my uncle's and aunt's. he never married because he was incarcerated for life. When he did get out of prison he committed suicide.

Now my mothers side of the family, which are the Baker's. Great Uncle Ernie was a popular person in the neighborhood. He was a manager of the A & P. Ernie also attended the Methodist Church at 5th and Cumberland Street in Philadelphia, Pennsylvania. Great Uncle Ernie never got a chance to marry because he enlisted into the Army. He went to war against Japan and died in a prison of war camp in the Philippines. My Great Uncle Billy served in the Navy. He married my Great Aunt Lois. They were Christians folks always doing things with their church. Great Uncle Billy worked for Bud Company which made the elevate train. He was an electrician for them. Great Aunt Lois was a homemaker. They never did have children. Both of them are passed away now, but they stayed married all way up to their death. Next is my Great aunt Virginia, which we call Aunt Jean. She worked for Nabiso and than a wash cloth company until she stopped working altogether. Than in her sixty she went on Public Assistance. She married once in her life and the one she married and the one she married left her. Aunt Jean never married again she stayed single. She died a horrible death by elevate train door trap her. Half of her body inside the other part outside being drag along to the next stop she die. My Great Uncle David was the youngest of my grand-mothers family. He never married but stayed living at home. When my great grand-mother died he took it hard. Before her death he did work, but he also got in trouble once in Texas and was incarcerated but got out. They say he had mental health problem. My Aunt Jean his sister supported him most of his life till he was in his late fiftys. Than he went on Public Assistance. My grand-mother Ruth was married to one who's last name was _____, but he left her. She also had two children from that marriage Richard and Barbara. My grand-mother remarried to a John who was Scottish. John worked for Yale Company while my grand-mother was a homemaker. They would argue a lot but always worked their differences out. My grand-mother died from a heartattach and passed away before my grand-father John. John lived by himself for a while than moved in with his one of his kids. For he two was married once before and children. He is passed away now. My Uncle Richard never married although he did live with women on occasion. He had a gambling problem throughout his life and he worked as a bouncer and bartender. Before his pass away he went back to church. Both the Stephenson and the Baker families are English descent.

My father was in the Navy and station in Philadelphia, Pennsylvania. I guess my mother like sailors for she married my father. Dad worked a lot different jobs. He worked for Stainless Press Steel but mostly my father was a truck driver. My mother worked on occasion but while she was married to my father she was a homemaker. My parents had five children together. Religion in our home was praying on holidays and special occasion. We went to church when my parent had the urge to go to church. Me for insistence did not know that Christ died to forgive my sins, nor for Him to be apart of my life. As far as morals go sure I knew not to steal, lie, but on sexual issues did not know only what school taught. My father taught me manners how to eat and behave in front of company. With my parent one has noticed their abusiveness toward one another. They fought and argued in front of us, even saw my father hit my mother and she hit him. Sometime they would yell about the North and the South. My mother would tell my father that the South lost and Yankee's won the war. Being that she was from Philly and a Northerner. I have heard on my fathers side from uncles and aunts that similar abuse problem existed between his father and mother. So after eleven years of marriage my father left with my mothers best friend. This woman bore him two children. Mary Sue my half-sister is now grown and married to Mark. They now have two children a boy and a girl. Than there is my half-brother Joe who is named after my dad. He is not married, and lives with a woman who has four children. One of them is my brothers. He also has another child by another woman. My mother was pregnant with my brother Mark when my father left her. She took his leaving very badly as well as the rest of us. After this my mother had a hard time adjusting to get things running right for us again. It took some time but we finally got on Public Assistance. We had to move in with my Aunt Jean, because my mother was now running around with other men. She also had two other children by two different men. Carl who is my half-brother is not married and now has six children by different women. His father was an orphan and when he was old enough went into the United States Marine Corps. He was married and had other children. But he also start running away with other women throughout his life. Than there my half-sister Domonique not sure if she got married to Steve or not, but they have two children. Her father also ran around with other women. Our family with it dysfunctional unhealthy behavior with the man running around with women and than my mother doing the same seems to have rubbed off on us. This reminds one of 2 Peter 2:14 "They have eyes full of adultery" with virtually every woman they meet. Their appetite for sins is never satisfied. My father remarried.

My sister Donna is the second sibling and she married at an early age. She wanted to get married to get out of the house and away from my mother. It just did work out that way, because she still did not leave until she in her twenties. She married a Richard, I even went to school with him for a short time. They had two children both girls. One is now married and the other is single. The one that is married does not have no children yet. Richard has passed away. My sister is still along that I know of. Joanne is the three sibling and she has been married twice. Her first husbands name was Richard and she named her first born Ricky. She also had another son by Richard. Her second marriage seems to be going well. Walter is the fourth sibling and he is not married. But he does have one child. Walter use to be a boxer but he no longer does it. He is like my father and loves to work. My brother Mark is fifth sibling. He is married and has one child. We were never taught biblical values. Where the Bible clearly affirms that both men and women are created in God's image and have equal value and dignity in God's sight and for the work of his kingdom on earth. We should not be abusive to those we say we love. Husbands and wives should share in responsibilities and help each other as partners in establishing a household and raising a family. There are some that do know the responsibilities in family but have not put God number in their lives. Some of my brothers including me, that in a marriage between man and woman commit to live with each other as husband and wife for life. In order for them to keep this commitment, both parties have to remain in the marriage. But when one party decides to leave the marriage for another partner, it becomes impossible for the remaining spouse to faithfully fulfill his or her commitment.

Than there is me, the first born of my parents, which both are pass away since my incarceration. Throughout my life I have been a failure as a son, brother, husband, and father. Roseanne is the mother of my son who is my first born. Roseanne is also my half-brother Carl's sister. They have the same father. I left Roseanne for another girl, which I did not even stay with long. Stayed with Roseanne about a year. Than there is Charlotte who I shacked up with for about five years. Her father worked for the fire department as an emergency medical technician. He was married and stayed married to his wife who was a homemaker. They had five children. Charlotte was married before me and had a son from her previous husband. Me and Charlotte had a one child together. Have not seen my daughter since 1983. Cheated on Charlotte with another woman. Me and this other woman did not stay long together because Roseanne set me up. Roseanne was staying down the block from this other woman. One night as I was going to the other woman's house Rose was outside her house and asked me in. And of course I went in and we had sexual intercourse, and the other woman found out, and that was the end of our relationship. Could I blame the woman no! Still with Charlotte, still cheating on went with Linda. Left Charlotte and married Linda. At first there was a lot of romance, and we both agreed that if we got married it was for keeps. Linda was never married but had a child, which was a girl. Her father and mother was divorce and had five children. Linda's father was a truck driver and her mother groomed dog for a living. Me and Linda stayed together for five years. Than Linda filed with the court a separation. I put Linda through hell took my belongs and left. But I just had to steal the car what a big mistake on my part. Then I finally made my way in the South. In Corinth, Mississippi found another woman. She was having marital problems with her husband. Bren left him to be with me. They had two girls, and Bren lost them because she choose to come with me. Bren's husband divorced her. As time went by she helped me get a divorce than we got married. My sexual habit got me trouble, and I did a wrong that really has taken its toll on others and me that I have hurt because of my sexual immorality. Having had sexual relationship with my step-daughter. I am now serving two life sentence because of my actions. If only I would have read and applied Matthew 5:27-28 where Jesus speaks on how lust is harmful. Acting out sinful desires is harmful in several ways: it causes people to excuse sin rather than to stop sinning, it destroys marriages, it is deliberate rebellion against God's Word, it always hurts someone else in addition to the sinner, sinful are more dangerous that sinful desires, and that is why desires should not be acted out. Nevertheless, sinful desires are just as damaging to obedience. Left unchecked, wrong desires will result in wrong actions and turn people away from God. To be faithful to your spouse with your body but not your mind is to break the trust so vital to strong marriage. Jesus is condemning not natural interest I the opposite sex or even healthy sexual desires but the deliberate and repeated filling of one's mind with fantasies that would be evil if acted out. Now I know how damaging it is for these action. This is not just a problem I deal with but also the men mention in this paper. I pray that we accept Jesus as Lord and follow His commandments, so that we do not walk in the lust of the eye nor flesh.

Another problem is listening. This was a problem with me in my relationships. I wanted to do more talking than listen. Being self-centered everything had to be about me. Instead of letting the other person share and be more open to their needs. In my relationships with the other party would feel that I didn't understand their feelings. One should have tried to identify the core motion they were experiencing and reflected on it letting them know you care. Showing more respect when it came to communication. Making a nonverbal and verbal expression a tone of voice and volume that it created a calm environment. Understanding one's spouse better. One has also noticed that the some of men left their responsibility of the family including my father. Seems he left it up to my mother to raise us without a man figure. Sure my mother made mistakes but she did try to straight herself up and do the best she could with us children. After all is said and do if I knew what I know now I would have give her the son she wanted and not be out for ones self but for others. This goes for the way I have treated my brothers and sisters, half-brothers and half-sisters, and people that have crossed my path. Hope my family forgives me because no matter what their my family and I forgive them even if they done something to me. Love is important in a family it makes us strong. My mother use to say you know I love you but never really show it. But I know deep in her heart she really did care about each of us because she did not abandoned us!

The best success on my family started with my childrens, nieces and nephews going to college to finish getting their education after highschool, which my brothers, sisters, and myself did not pursue the issue of continuing our education. Therefore, as me bing the oldest with four kids, my oldest were the first to get a bachelor in nursing, and next my second child; my oldes son, a bachelor degree in physical therapy. Also I have a niece that are very successful in cosmetologist.

Speaking of success in the pass on my family history I can go back only to my father on his ability to farm. Farming was what my father were a professional at when it came to planting any kind of seed, especially cotton, soybeans, vegetables, and fruits. My father had such good ethics in growing cotton and soybeans, plus his fruits and vegetables were tasty and delicious to everyone in the community and other farmers as well. Many farmers were so enthusiastic about my father's skills in farming they request for his assistance in growing their crops. Now, I say my father was successful in farming because he was one of a few black men that had over five hundred acres of land with no morer than a fifth grade education to manage his farm. That is also how my father got the resources to support his family and we were well taken care of.

My mother was a successful restauranteur and also one of the best cooks in the community, and just as my father was she had only a fifth grade education. My parents raised seven childrens well clothed, feeded, and Christian raising high school graduates. Those are my reasons for saying my parents were successful in their lives. Mother was also very devoted to going to church every Sunday, and making sure all my brothers and sisters were right there with her doing church service. My father was always working and wasn't to much of a church going person, so, very sudden he would attend church with us, unless it was a certain or special occasion like holidays such as Easter, Christmas, or funerals.

Even though, my family grew up in a Christian environment. As my brothers and sisters grew up and had families of their own, we kind of strayed away from church for a little while. I thank my aunt for guiding me back to church because of the pain and suffering I was going through in that time of my life. Now, in this situation I can say that I was successful in getting my family involved back in church membership. And the next year my family (brothers, sisters, their childrens and my children) was united to Rose Hill Missionary Baptist Church. My position in the church was an usher, and my brothers and sisters have also taking position as choir members, ushers, secretary, and what makes it even better is that the church is growing through my family.

The worst failure in my life besides me being incarcerated for the crime I committed, would be all the adultery and fornication that I committed growing up as a young man. Because as a grown man now I know that I was wrong in God's eyesight. The things I was doing was wrong because no man should go around spreading his seed to several other women having childrens by each one as I did. Please, don't get me wrong, I was taking care of my childrens even though I have four children by four different women. My first child was by my ex-wife out of wedlock, second child by a friend that was only a sex partner, third child was a girl involved with my best friend, and I became attractive to her, but not in love, and later found out she was pregnant with my child by DNA testing. My fourth child by another man's wife who pursued me like a beagle dog chasing a rabbit, and it didn't take long for that chase to go on because I loved myself some women and unprotected sex.

Therefore, I believe the cause of that failure in my life and family of orgin started on my mother side of the family with her father (my grandfather). My mother have twelve siblings, which my grandfather fathered by four different women and had a family. Two of those women, five childrens in each family, and two outside kids by the other two women. Now as I think of it my brother have kids by several other women, and I have a sister in the same catergory that my brother and I are in, that I consider to be a failure to my family.

A failure that I consider on my father side of the family is a habit of consuming to much alcohol. Which, I know have been passed down from my grandfather to my father, my brothers and my self. I have not seen this alcoholic problem with my sisters or any other female in the family, but many children by outside women or men's, and no outside children on my father's side, but they had assess to consume large amounts of alcohol.

Incidentally, the situation with my daddy and grandfather alcoholic problems have caused considerably amount of health problem in my family such as (kidney failure to dialysis, heart problems and diabetes to divorces), which I consider all to be a failure from drinking to much or having an excessive amount of alcohol. My grandfather pasted away from having a stroke and had diabetes. My father pasted away from having a heart attack, he was on dialysis machine three times a week, and taking insulin twice a day for diabetes. Excessive alcohol drinking was a failure to my father and grandfather health. On my behalf consuming alcohol excessive caused me to lose my family (ex-wife and first child) had serious financially problem, and involved with several other women. I actually believe that consuming alcohol excessively is what caused me to have a failure in marriage.

Changing from failure to success in my family, I reflect back on my brother in law and sister. How they have been successful in their business and thinking about expanding from Detroit to Huntsville, Alabama. Their two sons are also in the business with them owning their own trucks and travel all over the country. Actually it's a family business and they also have a daughter going to Alabama State majoring in business management to one day take over the business.

My sister, which is the second child of seven, has been in business running a delicatessen for over fifteen years which I believe is a skill she got from our mother as an experience on hand cook of all trades (Soul food, seafood, specialty on pizzas, bakery and desserts). She have also been a clerk for the county of eighteen years and training other people as well.

Dr. Hubbell I believe there has been more failure in my family and my self as I look back and write these failure in my family then success and I am disappointed in my family. Also as I look back and write these failure and success in my family of origin, Dr. Hubbell, I wish not to continue writing on the failure and success of my family orgin because there are no more I can share and I wish not to lie about any of it. Also, please accept what I have written even though I know you ask for ten pages.

Person 23

My family of origin will start with my grandparent. I do not know anything of my great-grandparents. I will also be favoring my dad's side due to the lack of knowledge for my mother's side. My mother's dad commited suicide when I was a baby and her mom we call me-mama. She lives in Gulfport and is unmarried. My dad's father we called Papaw. His name was Ray. He was originally from Ohio. He joined the Air Force and went into the engineering department. Sometime in the 40's he was moved down to Biloxi because of the Air Force. My dad's mother we call Mamaw. Her name was Opal and she was originally from North Mississippi. I'm not sure how she ended up in Gulfport. I always heard a story where she met Ray one night after heavy drinking. Not sure what to believe. Either way they met and got married. Sometime in the early 50's they had my aunt Brenda. Over the next five years they had another child, my aunt Gail, and my dad, Donald. The family of Welch resided in Gulfport. Papaw worked in Keesler Air Force base and my Mamaw was a housewife.

My mother's side includes two aunts and one uncle: Mitzi, Cindy, and Ricky. My mother's name is Vicky., their last name is Matthews. They also resided and most still reside in Gulfport.

My parents went to Gulfport High School. Sometime in their senior year, they got together. When it was time to get married they went to Alabama to elope. Her parents were against the marriage but my dad's parents attended the service. The Matthew's family always had a "my shit don't stink" attitude. This attitude still exists today. I just want to add at this time that because of my imprisonment, the Welch family is still in contact with me, not the Matthews. This also includes my mother and sister. Anyway, after they got married they resided in Gulfport.

October, 1976 my sister, Brandy, was born. Two years later, I was born. We had a normal child hood. My parents fought a lot but who doesn't. My dad was also an engineer but not in the military. My mother was an office worker. We were not poor, but we also was not rich. In those days you would call us middle-class. We lived in two houses from the time I was born to the fourth grade. I had a typical upgrowing with family holidays and reunions. On my mother's side I have seven cousins and my dad's side I have four cousins. Growing up me and my sister were closer to my dad's family.

When I was in the fourth grade we moved to Alabama because my dad got transferred. Living there was rough on me. I missed my friends and family in Gulfport. I still had my sister. While living in Alabama my dad starting having an affair with his receptionist. My mother found out and packed me and my sister up and we moved back to Gulfport. I have blocked out a lot of this due to hurt, but I will try to fill the gaps. In my tenth year of age, they got a divorce. The three of us moved to Long Beach, MS. My dad married the receptionist and moved to Atlanta. He then insisted on me and my sister calling her "step-mom". As you can guess, that was a problem and me and my sister loathed going up to Atlanta to visit. Sometime between then and my sixteenth birthday, they got a divorce and he moved back to Gulfport.

My mom got remarried when I was seventeen. My sister also got married at the same wedding. She was nineteen. My mom is still married to Dave and they reside in Biloxi. My sister had a boy, Austin, but got a divorce. She is remarried and lives in Hattiesburg. She has two kids: Austin and Gracie.

From my eighteenth birthday til my twenty-seventh year I resided from Long Beach, to Biloxi, to Gulfport. I followed my dad's occupation and worked as land surveyor in his engineer's office. During this time of growth me and my dad patched up our relationship. My sister on the other hand still resents him. I want to add at this time that I led my dad to Christ and he is my best friend in this place. Praise Jesus!

In 2005, my dad met a woman in the post office. They became friends. I'm not sure of their relationship but they wanted to match up me and her daughter, Beth. Christmas 2005 my dad invited Suzette (the woman from the post office) over to his house to help decorate the Christmas tree. He invited me and she invited her. I met my wife that night. From that moment forward we were unseperatable. We dated for four years and got married in 2009. Married life was great. We resided in Gulfport. In 2010 we bought a house and planned to start our family. In 2011, I was arrested and sent to prison. In 2012, we got divorced. I still love her to this day and wish things could be different.

Here it is 2015 as I write this. The only people that I remain in contact with is my dad's side of family. I love them and appreciate their support. I am currently praying for a revival of the other half. So, I guess you can say I'm 90% Welch and 10% Matthews.

I have been incarcerated since I was 19 years old. Most of my extended family I do not know. My mom and dad both raised me. My dad's name is Henry E. Sr. and my mom's name is Shirley J.. They are both in their latter years now. My dad is 74 and my mom is 68.

I have a sister named Catherine J. and she is 46 years old. My parents from my point-of-view are good parents. There was no alcohol abuse in the home and no drug abuse by either of my parents. However, me and my sister are a different story altogether.

My dad was raised in and around Vicksburg, as well as, my mom. All of my mom's brothers and sisters are currently residing in Vicksburg. Both of my parents are from rather large families. In my immediate family it is only me and my sister. I knew my moms brothers and sisters before I was incarcerated. However, now almost all of them have nothing to do with me.

My dad was not an educated man but he worked and provided a good living for his family. He was a towboat operator for as long as I can remember. He made a decent living and we lived in the middle-middle class. My dad, according to him, was raised poor. His dad moved him about from riverbank to riverbank. My granddad divorced my dad's mother and took him. My dad told me he never made it past the sixth-grade.

My mom she was orphaned when she was about 11 years old. She told me she grew up in an orphanage raised by a nanny. Her mom died and her dad was not able to provide for her. She met my dad at the age of sixteen and they were married. My dad was 25 at this time. My mom said she was pregnant at least five times and only carried the two of us. My mom was a high school graduate and worked at Shoe City as a manager. Mostly they were both present in the home when we were raised. My dad, because of his work schedule was gone for birthdays and Christmases, but he had to work.

I never graduated from high school either. I tried to join the military at the age of 18 with only a G.E.D. I was refused by the Marine Corps and not interested in the Army. As far as I know, no one in my family ever joined the military. My mom wanted me to graduated high school, she stated, "I would be the first male in the Stephens family to graduate from school." Her dreams were not fulfilled for me.

For the most part my family members supported me physically and emotionally. They disapproved of my alcohol use and tobacco use. However, my dad smoked cigarettes and I was rebellious toward any suggestion that I not use the substance. Some of my uncles and aunts used alcohol and cigarettes as well. I have at least one cousin that is currently incarcerated. I do not know for what though. Most of my aunts and uncles are dead now from cancer or emphysema. I am not aware if it runs in the family or not.

My sister graduated from high school but did not do anything with her life. She is currently disabled and on medication. She also has two boys and they are currently living with my parents. I believe that my parent's generosity is a crutch that was abused by me and my sister to a certain extent.

Currently, since my incarceration over the last 20 years, my parents have supported me financially, emotionally, and spiritually. They adopted my only daughter after my incarceration. Many people would have left their sons or daughters by now in my opinion. If my family has one flaw I desire to see fixed it was their lack of communication.

Person 25

Reading this autobiography of my life, you will see that I was pretty rough around the edges. I grew up on the west side of Jackson, MS. I am the second oldest of six, I have two sisters and three brothers, and I attended a county school outside of Jackson. I have always been a child that admired my father and tried to pattern my life after him, because he always made things look so easy. When I started school I couldn't talk very well. The other kids often made fun of me, so I didn't talk very much. I stayed at home for fighting. My dad would always try to help me speak better. He always say just take your time son. My dad is a very compassionate man. He puts his heart into everything. My dad taught me self control, how to deal with people, and when to dispence my anger. I started playing football in Junior high. I was a mean little fellow, because had been picked on at school and at home. A lot of times I felt the only friend I had was my dad. I got my first car at the age of fourteen. I drove everywhere. With that car came responsibility which was no problem because dad taught me to be just that. I learned to work and save money. I was taught that if a man don't work he shouldn't eat. Dad often repeated those words and my grandfather as well. I played high school ball and went on to play at J.S.U. I always had a dream of playing for the New Orleans Saints. It didn't work out though. I got married at the age of nineteen because my girlfriend was pregnant. My wife and I were blessed with three kids two boys and one girl. My wife and I separated after about 4 years. I remarried in two thousand five. I am currently married today. I ran the street, acted a fool, did drugs, and lived a secret life that soon came to light. I made a living driving a truck, I even started my own trucking business. I enjoyed having control over what I made and how much although it wasn't a good thing. I spent too much time away from home. Growing old I began to see my mistakes. June two thousand eight I was accused of rape a crime I could never commit. In less than a year later I'm in prison. I'm still fighting to get out, but not by myself. I have Jesus this time. I gave my life to Christ over a year ago that has been the best choice I could make. I've did time at Rankin and Green County. I'm currently at Parchman, MS learning all I can. I came in a lost broken man, I'll leave a new revived man.

Conclusion

The Parchman prison system has been radically changed over the years since the 1960s because of judicial action. When I was first introduced to the penitentiary as a visitor, the housing appeared to be inferior and guards with their guns left me with the impression that the motive for one's incarceration was punishment only—not punishment and rehabilitation.

When I returned in the 1970s as a Ph.D. student for research relating to prisoners at the pre-release center and then life after their release to their respective states (Mississippi, Alabama, Louisiana, Tennessee), I discovered improvements in the overall system. And then when I began teaching for the New Orleans Baptist Seminary at Parchman in 2001, I was again impressed with changes. Yet, I have deep sadness when I pass the maximum security unit. I realize that these persons are in this unit because of the risks they potentially present to the prison system if they were housed elsewhere.

I still have genuine feelings for those in maximum security for, after all, they are still persons. And when I pass the unidentified cemetery and particularly the new cemetery with individualized crosses, I realize that those who died in prison were without family members or any concerned extended family caring or noting their deaths. Even the newest cemetery strikes me with sadness for the same reason. No one seems to care. And when I read on their tombstones their prison numbers, I have the sad thought that they are known even after death by their numbers—if anyone should ever care.

The prison population (4,000) and the 7 units in which they are housed are generally viewed as housing violators deserving incarceration. I recognize and respect the judicial system; yet at the same time, I believe that from the Creator's point of view, they are still people—PRISONERS ARE PEOPLE.